ARMY BASIC TRAINING: BE SMART, BE READY

ARMY BASIC TRAINING: BE SMART, BE READY

Raquel D. Thiebes

Library of Congress Number: 00-193439
ISBN #:   Softcover   0-7388-5742-4

This book was printed in the United States of America.

To order additional copies of this book, contact:
Xlibris Corporation
1-888-7-XLIBRIS
www.Xlibris.com
Orders@Xlibris.com

CONTENTS

This book is dedicated in loving memory to my mother Inge, my family and to all the drill sergeants and trainees who have chosen to make Army Basic Training a part of their lives.

Note: The trainees' quoted comments throughout the book are true quotes by real trainees. The trainees' names have not been included to protect their privacy. The short italicized stories are real stories with fictional trainee names. The drill sergeants and cadre who have provided their names and comments are real.

On the cover: A drill sergeant is supervising a private firing an M203 grenade launcher downrange.

INTRODUCTION

Every year, thousands of young men and women join the Army. Even with the continued downsizing of today's Armed Forces, the recruiting quotas continue to demand more soldiers.

The Army is still one of the best places today to get a jump on life and a career. What other organization has all the benefits, training and leadership opportunities the Army has to offer? There isn't a company or corporation in the world that would hire you and be able to give you a better offer. Think for a moment why you want to join? Are you interested in the college money? Job skills? Benefits? The opportunity to see the world? Tradition? Whatever the reason, in order to become an enlisted soldier in today's Army, you will all start out your career in basic training.

Before you actually begin basic training, there are many factors you must consider. First, you must decide how long you want to serve. You can initially commit to as little as two years or as many as eight years. You can choose to serve in the active Army, the Reserves or the National Guard. The Army has over 250 job specialties, known as Military Occupational Specialties (MOS), ranging from a cook to an infantryman. The jobs open to you depend on the vacancies the Army currently has and how well you do on the Armed

Services Vocational Aptitude Battery (ASVAB) Test. This test is used to assess your skills and aptitudes and focuses on ten separate areas that include: general science, arithmetic reasoning, word knowledge and paragraph comprehension.

Once you have your test score, you'll be in a better position to negotiate what MOS you would like to be trained in. Do you want to make the Army a career or would you rather learn a skill or trade you can use in the civilian world? If you choose to be an infantryman, there isn't much of an equivalent job position in the civilian sector. Although you will still gain the confidence, leadership skills and self-discipline that can be applied to any career or job. If the Army has shortages in a particular MOS and you qualify, you may be eligible for an enlistment bonus up to $12,000.

If you're looking for money for college, the Army is the place to get it. The Montgomery GI Bill, combined with the Army College Fund can earn you up to $50,000 for college to use when you finish your Army commitment. While you're on active duty, you may be eligible to have the Army pay up to 75% of college tuition and fees for classes you take. Many soldiers take advantage of this by earning their degrees in their off-duty hours. If any of these ideas appeal to you, see your recruiter today for more information.

After you discuss the various options available to you with your recruiter, you will report to a Military Entrance Processing Station (MEPS). This is where you will have a physical exam, take mental qualification exams, talk with an Army guidance counselor and review all the options you have chosen. Only after this is completed, do you actually sign an enlistment contract that details your period of service, training you are to receive, and any other terms and guarantees.

If you're not quite ready to go to basic training right away, one of the options available to you is the Delayed Entry Program (DEP). This program guarantees your training, in writing, up to 365 days before you leave home. This can give you time to continue your education and to work for an advanced promotion. As a bonus, you can use this time to get physically and mentally ready and say good-bye to family and friends. While in this program, you can even earn your first promotion as a Recruiter's aide. This means, that if you refer two qualified high school seniors or graduates, who enlist in the Army, Army National Guard or Army Reserves, you'll enter the Army as a Private Two (E-2).

Basic training is generally a nine-week course. Again, this depends on whether you go to a unit that purely teaches basic training or one that teaches both basic training and advanced individual training. If you have to go to another unit for your advanced individual training (AIT), your basic training will be nine weeks long. If you are staying in the same unit for both stages of training, known as One Station Unit Training (OSUT), you will have only eight weeks of basic training. Both types of units have the same core curriculum for basic training. Every enlisted soldier goes through this same initial basic training. Officers in the Reserve Officers Training Corps (ROTC) and the United States Military Academy (USMA) at West Point receive similar training, although the focus here is more on leadership skills.

In observing trainees participating in basic training, it seems that many of the trainees are not prepared for the training. They either have the notion of a "killing machine" soldier or they are totally naive about the physical and mental stamina necessary to succeed. If you fall into either category, or somewhere in between, this book will help you prepare. If you are just curious what Army basic training is like, this book will enlighten you. If you decide to be a part of it, basic training is one of the most physically and mentally challenging experiences you will face in your lifetime. This book will give you a "leg up" on everything you need to know. If you still have questions after reading this book, please come by my website at http://www.armybasic.homestead.com to learn more, join a discussion forum or just make comments and ask questions!

CHAPTER 1:

GET PHYSICALLY FIT

You've probably heard plenty of horror stories about the physical abuse your body takes in basic training. If you are in fairly good physical condition when you arrive, your body will quickly adapt. Extensive physical exercise in the few weeks prior to your induction into basic training after years of inactivity is the gravest mistake you can make. You will only succeed in breaking your body down, and potentially creating stress fractures and injuries, especially in your lower extremities. Too many trainees experience the pain and frustration of stress fractures in their shins, hips and feet. In the first two weeks of training, there are inevitably six to ten soldiers on crutches per company, as a result of these stress fractures. The concept you need to remember is to develop your physical conditioning—gradually. Preferably, you should begin an exercise program at least three to six months before starting basic training. This chapter will put you on the right track. As with any new exercise program, ensure your healthcare professional has cleared you to begin exercising, especially if you are unaccustomed to any type of physical activity.

"Basic training to me was like taking a spoon full of cough medicine as a kid, hating the taste of it, but knowing that it is something you need. Coming into training, I was nothing but a couch potato, I loved to sit and watch TV everyday and sleep till about noon. After eight weeks of intense training though, I am more active and feel as if I can take on the world. After all the pain I have went through from physical training, being away from home, and not being a civilian, overall it has been a good pain. Since I have joined the Army I have seen nothing but improvement in my self-discipline, teamwork, abilities and confidence."

"I enjoyed the physical exercise that took place. I never realized how important exercise was until I came here."

In basic training, there are some basic events in which you must excel. The Basic Physical Fitness Test (BPFT) consists of three events: the push-up, the sit-up and a two-mile run. You will conduct extensive marches; wearing a Kevlar helmet, rucksack, weapon and boots, all weighing about 30 pounds. Many activities require upper body strength. There will be obstacle courses and rifle ranges that require a considerable amount of physical exertion. You will run almost every other day. Every day of your training will be marked by some kind of physical activity.

"Basic training for me was a challenge. I [have] done things that I thought I would never do in my life, for instance the confidence course. I'm very scared of heights and I never thought I would be so high up in the air that I had to get down the way I got up, but it made me a stronger and well-minded soldier. The only thing that got to me was the roadmarches, some privates walk slower than others plus, carrying something on our backs just made it worse."

THE BASIC PHYSICAL FITNESS TEST (BPFT)

The Basic Physical Fitness Test (BPFT) is an important test the Army uses to determine your level of physical fitness. The Army uses a point system to score the test. You are awarded a certain number of points according to your age and sex. The points reflect the number of repetitions within two minutes for sit-ups and push-ups. For the two-mile run, points reflect the time it took you to run two miles; the faster the run, the higher the points. In basic training, you are only required to achieve 50 points in each event. That's why it's called the Basic Physical Fitness Test. By the conclusion of advanced individual training (AIT), you must achieve 60 points in each event. This then is called the Army Physical Fitness Test (APFT).

Why are males and females given a different number of points for the same repetitions or time on the run? This is due to known physiological differences between men and women. The Army conducted extensive tests over a number of years, and these are some of the results. In comparing two 18-year-olds of different sexes, the Army found major physiological differences. Males have 50% greater total muscle mass based on weight than women. Women, on average, are 80% as strong. This gives the average male the advantage in strength, speed and power. Women have a higher percentage of body fat and a lower center of gravity. Males are built to run more efficiently with narrower hips and greater bone mass. A female's heart is 25% smaller than a typical male's, enabling the male to pump a greater volume of blood. Males also have 25-30% greater lung capacity which allows them to process oxygen more efficiently. Now this does not mean that every male and female falls into these two categories. These are just average findings that the Army has accepted and incorporated into its physical fitness plan and scoring system for the physical fitness test.

    Listed below are minimum and maximum standards for the physical fitness test for males and females in basic training. Go to the appropriate chart, and find your age in the far left-hand column. Look across to find the minimum/maximum number of repetitions needed for the push-up and sit-up, and the minimum/maximum times needed for the two-mile run. In order to pass the test, you must meet the minimum requirements. If you want to excel, you can reach for the maximums below. At the end of each cycle, the trainee with the highest score is given an award for his or her efforts.

PHYSICAL FITNESS TEST:
MALES MINIMUM/MAXIMUM STANDARDS

AGE	PUSH-UPS MIN/MAX	SIT-UPS MIN/MAX	TWO-MILE RUN MIN/MAX (minutes)
17-21	35/71	47/78	16:36/13:00
22-26	31/75	43/80	17:30/13:00
27-31	30/77	36/82	17:54/13:18
32-36	26/75	34/76	18:48/13:18

PHYSICAL FITNESS TEST:
FEMALES MINIMUM/MAXIMUM STANDARDS

AGE	PUSH-UPS MIN/MAX	SIT-UPS MIN/MAX	TWO-MILE RUN MIN/MAX (minutes)
17-21	13/42	47/78	19:32/15:36
22-26	11/46	43/80	20:36/15:36
27-31	10/50	36/82	21:42/15:48
32-36	9/45	34/78	23:06/15:54

Roadmarching

From the first day of training, the drill sergeants are already conditioning you to march longer and longer distances. Your first marches will be with limited gear, such as your BDU softcap and Load Bearing Equipment (LBE), which is a belt that carries your canteens and ammunition pouches. In addition, you will have a lightly packed rucksack. Distances will typically be less than a mile the first few weeks, to and from your classes. Most marches will be with your company marching together in a formation, rather than tactically. This is the time to start breaking in your boots and toughening up your feet. If you worked on conditioning your feet before you came, you'll be that much more ahead.

By the third week, you'll wear the heavier Kevlar helmet, carry your weapon and pack a loaded down rucksack. The march distances average two to twenty kilometers and are conducted tactically. As you become better conditioned, your body will gradually adapt to the stresses of these heavier loads and longer distances.

Obstacle and Confidence Courses

You will participate in at least two major obstacle courses while in basic training. One, the Physical Endurance Course (PECS) will not only test your stamina, but also your ability to negotiate obstacles individually. In full combat gear, you will move through a course at a quick pace, running from obstacle to obstacle. You'll find yourself climbing cargo nets, crawling through tunnels, negotiating rope bridges, climbing up ropes and jumping over walls.

The Confidence Course is more of a group effort, where you

RAQUEL D. THIEBES

negotiate large obstacles with the help of your fellow trainees. Many obstacles involve climbing to heights of over 40 feet, using teamwork to help each other up. The course promotes teamwork and confidence. Without good upper body strength, you may find yourself having a considerable amount of difficulty on this course.

Soldiers working together to negotiate this tower obstacle from the Confidence Course. Notice that the soldiers can only reach each level by boosting each other up, instilling a sense of teamwork.

"I enjoyed the confidence course. For somebody afraid of heights, that course was real tough, but by the time I completed it, I felt I could accomplish anything."

DAILY LIFE ON THE RANGES

After the second week of training, a lot of your time will be spent on ranges, away from the barracks area. There will be many times, when you are in a fighting position or foxhole, waiting for commands from the drill sergeants as you battle the elements. Whether the hot blazing sun or frigid arctic wind, you will train outside to some extent. This in itself can lead to physical exhaustion. Other ranges, such as the Fire and Maneuver Course, involve negotiating obstacles, firing at targets, running from cover to cover—all while wearing a heavy protective flak vest. The grenade range includes not only throwing numerous practice grenades, but also participation in a grenade qualification course—again physically challenging. There will be many days when you will be utterly exhausted from all the physical activity. Being physically fit will help you cope.

An instructor and a trainee crouch behind the wall as the explosion rocks the earth from a grenade the trainee just threw! In addition to the rifle ranges, this will potentially be the most dangerous thing you will do in basic training.

"For myself, the best part of basic training was qualifying with my M16A2 Rifle. The satisfaction of shooting expert made me feel proud to be a soldier. The work that we had to do with the simulators, I think, helped to make me a better shooter. Travelling to the different ranges and having to pass each challenge was fun and exciting."

"The grenades gave me more confidence and trust in myself and my battle buddies."

"I actually fell asleep cleaning my rifle after the Individual Tactical Training (ITT) Day. The course was so muddy and my rifle was caked in mud. It took me hours to clean it. To make matters worse, my knees and elbows were killing me from all the crawling."

IN AND AROUND THE BARRACKS

In addition to your physical training sessions, marching, firing and negotiating obstacles, you may find yourself working out in your "free" time. This may be done voluntarily or directed by a drill sergeant. Drill sergeants sometimes take time throughout the day to discipline trainees through physical exercise, or they might work with you to improve your form on push-ups or sit-ups. In the evenings, it's not unusual to see trainees assisting each other in improving their physical fitness test scores.

"Thanks to some of the other trainees in my platoon, I was able to pass my physical fitness test. If they hadn't pushed me to practice my sit-ups, I would have never made it."

PHYSICAL FITNESS TRAINING IN SUMMER AND WINTER

Whether you are going to basic training in the summer or winter months, physical fitness training sessions will be fairly similar. You will do the same type of exercise whether it's winter or summer. You will run even when it is cold outside and the sweat is forming icicles on your hat. In the summer, you may be instructed to carry your canteen while running and physical fitness sessions may be conducted in the earlier hours when it's cooler.

There's nothing more disheartening than waking up, looking outside and seeing a heavy layer of frost or snow blanketing everything. If you're going to attend basic training at Ft Sill or Ft Leonard Wood in the winter months, you are in for a very cold training session. It's not unusual for you to wear long underwear beneath your physical fitness uniform. Inevitably, most drill sergeants will tell you exactly what to wear. If you put too many layers on, you could easily become overheated, especially on the days that you go for long runs. You'll also wear gloves and a knit cap to stay warm if necessary. Sometimes you'll get "lucky" and have physical training sessions indoors, but don't think it will be any less strenuous. It's usually more exhausting. On the average, very few physical training sessions will be canceled due to weather.

In the summer, it gets extremely hot at all the basic training posts. Your company will have equipment to measure not only the temperature but also the humidity levels. Individual companies carry with them a "wet bulb", which measures these levels. Once the temperature/humidity reaches a certain point, training must slow down and in some cases must stop altogether. It can be pretty frustrating, not to complete your training for the day, because of the heat. Be prepared to drink a lot of water and to sweat like you've never sweated before. Almost all of your physical fitness sessions will be scheduled in the early morning to beat the heat in the summer months.

FOCUS ON THESE FIVE AREAS

Okay, so now you have an idea what types of activities you'll be doing and have a pretty good idea what happens during the physical fitness test. Before you get to basic training, concentrate on the areas listed below:

1. Running

•This is not something you can master within a few days. You need to gradually build up your stamina to be successful. Combining slow long distance runs with sprints is the only way you can increase your stamina and speed for the fitness test and other events in basic training.

2. Marching and Wearing Boots/Wearing a Rucksack

•Become comfortable wearing a rucksack with weight on your back. Take up hiking. Many trainees have never worn anything but tennis shoes their whole lives. This makes it extremely difficult to adjust to wearing boots. Take walks wearing boots. They don't necessarily have to be Army boots, but they should be sturdy hiking-type boots. Wearing these boots will toughen up your feet. Too many trainees limp around with painful blisters that could have been prevented had they only worn boots regularly before coming to basic training.

3. Do Moderate Weight Training

•You must have good upper body strength to do well. If you're familiar with weights, by all means, start training. If you are a beginner, ensure you have someone experienced help you or follow a plan approved by your physician and a fitness professional. Even home videos will help you get into better shape than you are now. Weight training will enable you to carry heavier loads. It also increases your ability to do well on the Basic Physical Fitness Test (BPFT).

4. Practice Proper Form Doing Push-ups and Sit-ups

•One of the biggest challenges you will face is using improper form when doing push-ups. This is especially true for females who generally have weaker upper body strength. When you do an incorrect push-up, it is not counted during the physical fitness test. Improper form takes away those points you really need to pass that test! Build up your lower back muscles, so you can hold your body in a generally straight line without sagging in the middle while you are doing the push-up. Practice going all the way down, until your upper arms are parallel with the floor. Again, if you don't go down far enough, the repetition will not count. Have someone you trust check out your form or use a mirror. The push-ups you might have done on the football team in high school may not be to the Army standard. Have your recruiter check out your form!

- One of the biggest mistakes people make when practicing sit-ups is to do them on a hard surface. When practicing sit-ups, always use a padded surface. Doing them on a hard surface may injure your tailbone. When coming up, make sure your hands stay clasped behind your head; don't pull on your neck to pull yourself up as this could cause a neck injury. Keep your buttocks on the ground throughout the motion and raise your upper body to where your back is vertical to the ground. Then lower your body until your shoulder blades touch the ground. Your knees will be bent at about a 45-degree angle. You'll have someone holding your feet during the test, so practice with someone holding your feet or anchor them under something. The sit-up is not only a test of abdominal strength, but also your hip flexor muscles. You may practice other abdominal exercises, but the only way to improve your sit-ups, is to actually do them the same way described above.

5. Learning to Throw
- Throwing live and practice-type hand grenades are both graduation requirements. It's a good idea to show up on the grenade range having at least learned how to throw a baseball or softball about 45 feet. Now is the time to learn before you become distracted by the sounds of shrapnel zinging around you from grenades that didn't go far enough. Make sure you throw the ball in an arc, like a long pass in football. Aim at a point in the sky so the ball travels up and then back down again. Avoid throwing the ball in a straight line. There's nothing more nerve-wracking or embarrassing than not graduating basic training with your peers, because you couldn't throw a grenade properly. It can happen.

RAQUEL D. THIEBES

Trainees demonstrating the proper form in throwing a grenade.
This will be what is expected of you.

Start a physical training program about three to six months before you start basic training. Focus on increasing your running ability, and be able to do the minimum correct push-ups and sit-ups for your age group when you arrive. Work on upper body and abdominal strength. Get someone with a fitness background to help you. Some recruiters take the time to conduct physical fitness sessions for their enlistees. It's well worth it for you to go and will save you some heartache later. In the few months before basic training, wear boots; practice hiking with a rucksack on your back. Keep these tips in mind, and you'll be ready.

YOUR DAILY FITNESS PLAN

Following these steps will increase your fitness level and prepare you for basic training. Again, ensure you have your physician's approval before you begin this or any other exercise program. The ideas, procedures and suggestions in this chapter are not intended as a substitute for consulting with your physician. All matters regarding your health require medical supervision. Whether you are a beginner or someone familiar with fitness training, use this plan as a guide on your way to total fitness.

WATCH WHAT YOU EAT AND FOLLOW A HEALTHY LIFESTYLE

In addition to the physical activity you must do before basic training, you also have to monitor your eating habits. The way you eat and what you eat have a major impact on your ability to improve your physical conditioning. Follow the USDA food pyramid, cutting down on fats and sweets. Your daily fat intake should be no more than 30% of your total caloric intake for the day. Load up on green, leafy vegetables, pasta, rice and breads. Try to stay away from sweet cakes, doughnuts, cookies and chips. Once you start eating healthier, your body naturally steers away from craving sweet, fatty and salty foods.

Condition yourself to drink plenty of water. The old adage that says to drink six to eight glasses of water a day still holds true! This will help keep your body well hydrated and will flush out all the toxins in your body. Get accustomed to drinking water now, especially if you don't like the taste. You won't be able to grab a soda or some other beverage whenever you like in basic training. In fact, you will rarely even see a can of soda! Practice carrying a one-quart water bottle around with you all day. Take small sips throughout the day, instead of drinking it all at once. Refill it once sometime during the day, and continue drinking!

Throughout basic training, drill sergeants will have scheduled "water drinking" sessions. A drill sergeant will have you take out your canteen, and you will start drinking. Be prepared for water that is lukewarm with a hint of the taste of plastic. Once you are done, you are required to hold the empty canteen upside-down over your head. No one will be allowed to go on a break or continue training, until everyone is done. If you did not take your sips throughout the day, you'll find yourself drinking the contents of your canteen all at once. It can also be pretty stressful, having the rest of the trainees waiting for you to finish. If you drink water now on a regular basis, it won't be that new to you in basic training.

If you use tobacco or drink alcohol, stop now. No alcohol or tobacco products are allowed. During training, you just don't need the extra pressures of going into withdrawal. You will already have enough things to worry about, without craving tobacco or alcohol. You may think it's hard to do now, but think ahead how much harder it will be in basic training. Quitting "cold turkey" is not for everyone.

If you are taking any kind of drugs, stop now. You will be drug tested during various stages of your new Army career, even before you ever start basic training! There is no mercy in the Army for those using drugs. Rest assured, you will most likely be discharged immediately.

ESTABLISHING YOUR BASELINE FITNESS LEVEL

Start out by having your recruiter, physical fitness teacher, or friend (or you can do it yourself) give you a physical fitness test to assess exactly where you stand. During the physical fitness test, you will always do push-ups first, followed by sit-ups and then the 2-mile run. Start out by doing as many correct push-ups as you can in two minutes. Proper form is very important. You cannot drop to your knees or reposition your hands or feet by lifting them, although you can slide your hands if necessary. There are only two authorized rest positions while doing push-ups. If needed, you can sag your belly in the middle or raise your buttocks in the air, giving your body a V-shape. You cannot rest by bending your knees and putting your body weight on your legs. Take a few minutes and then do correct sit-ups for two minutes. You cannot rest in the down position, lying on your back, although you can rest in the "up" position. Your legs must remain at a 45-degree angle, and your hands must stay clasped behind your head throughout the two minutes. Your buttocks must stay on the ground the entire time. Rest again for a few minutes and stretch your legs before you run. It's best to run your first test on a ¼-mile track, where you can see how much time it will take you to run each lap. You'll find it easier to pace yourself on a track. For example, if you want to run the test in 16 minutes, you know that each lap cannot take you more than two minutes on the average (8 laps x 2 = 16). If you're a beginner, you will most likely find yourself doing a lot of walking at first. That's okay. Walk at a quick pace and start running again as soon as you catch your breath. It's not unusual for a non-runner to have a time of 30 minutes at the end of the two miles. This will improve dramatically in a few weeks. Remember the number of repetitions for push-ups and sit-ups, plus your two-mile run time. Record the figures to use later.

Trainees pushing their way through the first part of the test. The male trainee in the foreground is allowing his body to sag in the middle, with only his feet and hands actually touching the ground. The male trainee in the upper left-hand corner is holding his body up in a "v" shape. These are both authorized rest positions while doing the push-up. The female trainee in the middle of the photo has been terminated and can no longer do any more push-ups for the test, as she is resting on her knees.

YOUR PHYSICAL CONDITIONING PLAN

Step 1:

My First Physical Fitness Test (Date):	
Push-up Repetitions:	
Sit-up Repetitions:	
Run time:	

Step 2: Improving Push-ups & Sit-ups (Monday, Wednesday, Friday)

Now that you have a baseline score, you are ready to start improving your fitness level. Your fitness training will consist of two main parts: push-up/sit-up improvement and running improvement.

This particular workout should be done on three non-consecutive days per week. The focus here will be on push-ups and sit-ups. You can still do some sort of cardio-respiratory exercise such as running, walking, biking or stair-stepping to warm-up. Before you start any kind of exercise though, spend about five minutes stretching!

Push-ups:
a. # of repetitions from your fitness test: _____
b. Divide # of repetitions by 3: _____
Sit-ups:
c. # of repetitions from your fitness test: _____
d. Divide # of repetitions by 3: _____
Schedule for Push-up/Sit-up Improvement:
Important: Remember to rest for 30 seconds to one minute between each set!
First Push-up Set ("b" from above): _____
First Sit-up Set ("d" from above): _____

Second Push-up Set ("b" from above): _____
Second Sit-up Set ("d" from above): _____
Third Push-up Set ("b" from above): _____
Third Sit-up Set ("d" from above): _____

Doing push-ups and sit-ups this way causes you to reach what is called "muscle failure". This just means that you break your muscles down the farthest you can, which will in turn build them up that much stronger. You will feel some discomfort, called the "burn", but this is not harmful. If you feel outright pain at any time, stop and get checked out by a physician. Focus on using proper form for as long as you can. At some point during the push-up set, you will find you can no longer hold or raise your body up. This is a good sign. Continue to do push-ups while on your knees until you've completed the set. Again, do the sit-up sets as described above. If you at any time cannot do a sit-up correctly, pull yourself up by your hands. At the end of each set, you should feel as if you couldn't possibly do one more repetition.

After you've completed one week of push-up and sit-up improvement, add three to four repetitions per set each following week. Once you have added twenty repetitions to each set, take a fitness test again and start over with the new numbers. Now you'll be well on your way to improving your score and becoming more physically fit. If you are advanced or need more variety, you can change your hand positions with each push-up and sit-up set. You can place your hands shoulder width apart for the first set of push-ups, farther apart for the second and touching together for the third set. For the sit-up, you can have your hands clasped behind your head for the first set, across your chest for the second, and alternating going up on each side for the third. This is the quickest way to build muscle endurance and is geared towards getting you in shape for the fitness test. If you have very poor upper body strength and feel you will have trouble carrying a rucksack, rifle or completing any of the other activities in basic training, consult your recruiter for some extra tips. Additional weight training may be necessary.

Step 3–Running Improvement (Tuesday, Thursday and Saturday)

Your running program should be conducted three days a week, but not on the days you worked push-ups and sit-ups. This will give you one day of rest a week. One running day will focus on sprinting and increasing your speed. The other two running days will focus on your endurance.

Run time:

e. Time it took you to run the two miles on the fitness test:

_____

f. ¼-mile run time (divide "e" by 8 and subtract 4 seconds):

_____

g. Walking/Jogging Time (double "f"): _____
   Sprint Day (Thursday):
   •Sprint/Run ¼ Mile or One Lap _____minutes (f)
   •Walk/Jog ¼ Mile or One Lap _____minutes (g)

Start out by doing four sets of each, running a lap and then walking a lap. A set consists of a run lap and a walk lap. If you are more advanced, you can sprint a lap and then jog the next lap. Once you are able to do eight sets with little difficulty, retest yourself over the same two-mile course. Start over again using the new times.

Endurance Days (Tuesday and Saturday):

On the other two running days, you will try to run at the same pace for one to three miles, no matter how slow it is. On these days you should try to run over different types of terrain, including hills. If you live in a flat area, be creative and use stairs or the steps at a local high school track. If you're not sure of the distance, drive the route beforehand with your car to get a better idea. Many cities also have running clubs that already have various routes planned out. You will gradually see that your running time will decrease the more you increase your distance. Of course this doesn't happen overnight, but you will see improvement fairly quickly. Again, stretching before and after every run is important.

Ideally, you should start this plan six months before basic training, but it will also work well only a few months out. Keep in mind that you can only be successful if you follow the plan faithfully. There will be days when you feel too sore to continue, but you really must keep at it to see improvement. If you are not seeing any improvement then you are not following the plan correctly.

CHAPTER 2.

GET MENTALLY PREPARED

You've read about the physical preparation necessary to do well, but the equally important mental preparation cannot be neglected. Most privates are away from home for the first time in their lives. Others are leaving a spouse and children at home who are counting on them for financial support. Some come from a community, where they may not have been exposed to people of other races and ethnic groups. Some males have never worked closely with females and vice versa. A considerable number of trainees continuously rebelled against their parents and any other type of authority while they were at home. Some trainees are shy, quiet and have been sheltered their whole lives by their parents. Now can you imagine what happens when you have such a large, diverse group of people, coming together and living, sleeping and working together for eight weeks!

"Overall, the basic training experience for me was well worth signing up. The things that we/I really enjoyed was getting to know and cope

with other people, putting aside our differences and being able to live as a unit."

"It's hard to wake up at 4:00 am to do physical training, to 'get dropped and smoked' for somebody else. These things show you how to work together as a team . . . When a person from a different race, state or country comes to you and helps you, that's when you know there is something special about it. It motivates you and makes you feel like you're in the right place."

THE INITIAL SHOCK

One thing you must understand as a new Army trainee, is that there is a reason for everything that is done in basic training. Your first impressions might include fear, confusion, surprise, anger, defeat, frustration or loneliness when you report to your basic training company. All these feelings are perfectly normal and expected. As soon as you get off the cattle truck, a large vehicle resembling a truck that transports cattle, the drill sergeants are yelling at you to line up and to get ready for shakedown. Trainees are running every which way, and everywhere you turn a drill sergeant is right in your face, telling you what to do.

THE BATTLE BUDDY CONCEPT

The first two weeks of basic training are the toughest. The drill sergeants "highly encourage" you to work together as a team. At this early stage, stress levels and anxiety, nevertheless, are high. You are expected to come together with the other trainees and to develop a sense of teamwork. There are no individualists in basic training. Once you arrive at your basic training unit you are assigned what is called a battle buddy. This is a trainee of the same sex as you who will commonly be referred to as your Siamese twin. You will do everything together! Now this may sound a little like kindergarten, but this idea works for all ages! You both will be encouraged to help each other throughout training and to watch out for each other's safety and well-being. You will quickly learn that you will get "credit" for everything your battle buddy does or fails to do!

"When I first began to consider joining the Army last year, I was very naive on what it was all about. The main reason I decided to enlist was to gain some discipline and learn some skills to further my career ambitions. I wasn't living up to my potential and that was very demoralizing. When I finally arrived at Ft. Leonard Wood, I was in for a rough awakening. At the time I was 230 lbs, a chronic smoker, and unaccustomed to any type of physical activity. I had smugly assumed that doing a few push-ups the month before I departed would be enough to shape me up!! The drill sergeants soon showed me the error of my assumption. If you had asked me in the first two weeks to describe basic, I would have replied, 'Hell on Earth'. I had never worked so hard in my life. I was in constant pain, and the other two privates my size were removed from training within days. No one, including myself, expected me to survive to Phase II. My Diagnostic Physical Fitness Test score was a whopping 14 points combined!"

Even though you are assigned a battle buddy, it is up to you to make it work. In light of the trainee abuse cases, which occurred at various Army basic training posts in the past, this concept did not always work. Not enough emphasis was placed on the battle buddy concept. For example, in the past, a battle buddy might have disappeared during "free time" or after "lights out". If you have any knowledge of what your buddy is doing, you may also be held accountable. When in doubt, do what you feel is right. If at anytime, you feel uncomfortable alerting your drill sergeant to any problems you might encounter, there are other avenues for you to follow discussed later in this chapter.

AFTER YOU'VE
BEEN HERE A FEW WEEKS

Stress will continue to be a part of every basic training day. Why does the Army create so much stress? You are subjected to stress, because it's the closest experience a soldier can go through without being in an actual combat environment. Think about it. If you can't manage stress in basic training, do you think you'd be able to handle the much higher stress level in combat?

"Since the beginning of our introduction to the Army, stress had been in presence. It started out with reception. We received many shots, which all were painful. Afterwards came 'shakedown'. This frightened many people as well as me. For the rest of my training my days and nights, I spent them fighting myself to keep going . . . I had to push myself to the limit. Part of me wanted to quit and the rest fought for me to stay on my feet and always motivated."

"This step was one of the best I have taken in my life. Basic Training was difficult more so on me mentally than anything else."

During the third and fourth week, there is a marked change in trainees' behavior. They actually begin to work together allowing the drill sergeants to ease up the pressure a little. Most of the trouble-makers (those resisting authority) are either working together with the others by now, or they've been weeded out. A lot of the trainees who are being discharged for a variety of reasons have been identified and removed from training (RFT). Trainees removed from training are separated from the rest of the privates in the company and spend their time doing administrative duties until they leave the unit and are discharged.

At this point in time, there are still a few privates in the company having problems adjusting. The mental health office even has a name for this condition, which is know as an "adjustment disorder". It is perfectly normal to feel this way and counselors, chaplains, drill sergeants and other cadre continue to counsel and assist trainees throughout the rest of the training.

MISSING TOO MUCH TRAINING

Walking by any marching formation, you may see a group of privates hobbling behind on crutches or on "code", who are missing training. A "code" is a restriction given to a private by a doctor or physician's assistant from the troop medical clinic. These restrictions are written on a profile sheet, limiting the soldier's physical activity. For example, a trainee with a sprained ankle may be put on a "code" to walk at his own distance with no running or marching for seven days. If you fall into this category, it's easy to get depressed, because you tend to miss a lot of the scheduled training and often feel left behind. Most companies identify you as a "code" by requiring you to wear a small tag on your uniform, detailing your restrictions. This prevents you from participating in any activities that may violate your "code". If you are out of the training loop too long, there is a chance you may be "new started" and reassigned into another unit to receive the training you missed and then to graduate with that unit at a later date. One of the best ways to stay off "code", is to refrain from overtraining right before you get here. If you do overtrain, you will show signs of stress fractures around the third week of training. The only treatment for stress fractures is continued rest, which you cannot afford here. You can't afford to miss a single day! There are no sick days in basic training!

THE BEST PART OF BASIC TRAINING

Trainees seem to find the last four weeks of training the most enjoyable. They actually begin to feel like soldiers, and feel more comfortable with Army customs and the military environment. What they've learned starts to come together and, they start forming lasting friendships with their fellow privates. Sure, they still miss their families and friends, but they feel they have a second family in the Army. They realize they are getting good training which steadily increases their confidence level. The drill sergeants don't seem quite as tough and the privates find a new type of respect for them. Of course, graduation and the sense of accomplishment seem closer too. They believe, and rightly so, that if they can get through this, they can get through anything.

I hope you're not afraid of heights! This will be you too, negotiating one of the high towers on the Confidence Course.

"I worked harder than I have ever worked in my life and enjoyed it
. . . Basic Training has taught me to be more outgoing and a stronger
person—both mentally and physically. Before I joined the US Army, I
was more timid and relaxed. I now am able to speak under pressure
more comfortably and with confidence"

"I began to realize that my drill sergeants weren't dropping me to be
mean, but because I needed twice as much physical training as the other
privates. That's when my morale began to improve. As a whole, the
company was beginning to solidify and become a unit. It was extremely
exciting to be a part of it. As Phase III kicked in, I was a different
person than when I arrived. I had lost 35 lbs and I was a lot healthier
than two months earlier. I felt a great deal of pride in my accomplish-
ments and those of my platoon and company. One of the best feelings I
will take from basic is that I stuck with it instead of quitting. I would
be lying if I said there weren't days I wanted to throw in the towel, but
I never once voiced those feelings."

How to Focus

During the in-briefing on the first day of training, trainees are asked
to remember why they enlisted. People join the Army for a variety
of reasons. Some join for the college money; others are in it for
adventure and travel. Perhaps some just want to start a new career
or learn a skill. Maybe a relative was a soldier and they would like to
follow in their footsteps. Maybe just a better paying job is in order.
Some want to prove that they can make it on their own. I've even
seen trainees who were literally kicked out of their parents' homes.
Now think about why you joined or want to join the Army. One
technique used to focus on your goals, is to write down your reasons for joining on a piece of paper and then to stick that paper in
your hat. Whenever you feel depressed or want to quit, get out your
piece of paper to remind yourself why you're here. That piece of
paper becomes well worn. It is always within arm's reach and

becomes a sort of good luck charm. You will find many days when you are ready to quit, as will everyone else. Keep your goals in mind to help you get over those low points.

WHERE TO GO FOR HELP

It also helps to talk about your fears and frustrations. You have your battle buddy to talk to. He is in the same situation as you! Even though you may be afraid of your drill sergeants initially, don't be afraid to approach them. There is nothing they haven't heard, especially if it's a problem from home. Even if you have problems at home, they can help. Occasionally, a trainee will have a death or major illness in the family during their training. It can usually be arranged for the trainee to return home for a few days. You must remember though that missing too much critical training could put you into a position of restarting into another company. Each case is handled individually.

"The drill sergeants in my company were a lot more relaxed than I expected. Of course I was scared to death of them, but I very rapidly grew to trust them. They really are more like teachers than I expected. I rarely felt threatened to ask a question and always received an answer. I thought that most of the time they were fair and did not ask too much."

Another great resource available to you is the battalion chaplain or any of the other clergy assigned to your basic training post. Your battalion chaplain may be one of any given religion but also is able to provide access to most of the major religions. There may be times when you feel too shy to see your drill sergeant or maybe you suspect your drill sergeant of some wrongdoing. Some trainees have found their chaplain/priest/rabbi a great sounding board. Everything discussed is strictly confidential, unless there is a threat of suicide or harm to another person. Your chaplain may choose to approach your commander about the issue, with your permission, to come up with a solution. Otherwise, he can approach the commander with generalities if this may be a systemic problem within your unit.

Going to religious services is the answer some need to cope with their new environment. Every basic training post has an extensive schedule of religious events. There are services and activities for many different religions, whether you are Protestant, Catholic, Jewish or Moslem. Even if there are no clergy from your particular faith available at your post, you will be provided the time and the resources to practice your faith. All Army clergy are familiar with many different religions and are required to provide support for all the major religions represented in their command. You may see Moslems, Buddhists and soldiers of other religions train successfully, yet still follow their faith. Going to church is a great release from the constant demands of training.

Sometimes, learning to adjust to a new environment is easier when you know someone is there to help with your financial problems. Many anxieties trainees have are a direct result of money problems at home. The Army has numerous agencies to assist you in developing a budget and can provide interest-free loans if you qualify. Your drill sergeant can make an appointment for you to see a financial counselor if you request it.

Mental health care professionals are also available to you for counseling sessions. You can schedule your own appointments through your drill sergeant, or your drill sergeant may schedule an appointment for you if he thinks you need help. The Reserve and National Guard soldiers are lucky to have liaison personnel to provide regular counseling as needed.

Some trainees cope well by having some time to themselves. After "lights out" in the evening, some privates cope by crying into their pillows as a kind of release. Some soldiers reflect to themselves while on fireguard duty or spend a little extra time in the latrine. There is nothing wrong with these coping techniques. Whatever works, use it! The best way to stay motivated and to have a positive attitude is to talk with one another. Talk to each other and get positive reinforcement from home in letters and phone calls.

The Battle Buddy from Korea

PVT Terring had a battle buddy from Korea, who had real difficulty understanding what was going on, because of the language barrier. PVT Terring, when he first arrived, had many problems coping with this new environment. He spent a lot of time either crying or lashing out. He was extremely homesick. Sometime in the second week, PVT Terring exuded a lot more confidence. He also seemed to volunteer for everything. We all wondered what turned him around. Later we discovered he took it upon himself to do everything in his power to get his battle buddy through basic training. It became a mission for him. He told his commander during graduation, that he realized he was being selfish. Most of all, he saw his battle buddy in real need for help. He showed him how to do the tasks in the evening and repeated what was taught in class. He eventually began to feel confident, as if he was the teacher, and actually forgot about himself and his own fears.

Accept the fact that you are entering a new, more structured environment than home. Realize that you are not the only one stressed out and afraid. Even if other soldiers don't show it, most are just as scared and unsure of themselves as you are. Help other trainees, and they'll want to help you. Tell your family and friends to send encouragement through their letters. Talk with your fellow soldiers for support. Use the support sources the Army has available, such as a chaplain, priest, liaison personnel or mental health counselors. Talking with one of these individuals is not frowned upon. In fact, it is encouraged if you need it. Once you graduate, no one will know you needed some additional support during basic training. Don't be embarrassed; you're not the first one to ask for help. Keep in mind what your goals are in joining the Army. By the time you arrive at your basic training company, the Army has already invested thousands of dollars in you. It's important for the Army to help you get through this difficult time, but you have to want to succeed yourself. No one can do the training for you. Try to stay positive always!

"My first few weeks here were very frustrating and confusing. I felt uncomfortable in a new environment, new people and the drill sergeants. I wanted to escape it all. However, I talked with a lot of my

peers, and I found out that they were experiencing the same feelings and thoughts as I had . . . I've learned how to communicate with people of all ethnic backgrounds. I've gained knowledge on how to talk with people without using my hands. Confidence, pride, dedication and teamwork have all become a part of my person. I wrote home plenty of times and my parents tell me they see a difference in me. They tell me I have matured tremendously, and I have the Army to thank for that. Plenty of times I didn't want to get up in the morning, or do physical training . . . Having no choices matures a person quickly."

CHAPTER 3.

YOUR PACKING LIST

It never fails. During pickup, when you are transported to your training company, many trainees strain under the weight, trying to lug around two large suitcases. Some trainees are surprised to discover that everyone must carry their own gear. Travel lightly! Not only will you have to carry your civilian bag from home, but also your military duffel bag full of military issue items. These items include such heavy items as your boots, dress shoes and uniforms. Even if your suitcase has wheels, the drill sergeants will probably make you carry it. The best type of suitcase you can bring is a large, sturdy gym bag with two short handles and a shoulder strap. This is all you will need. If you must carry something separately, bring a lightweight portfolio or large envelope for your important papers and documents.

CONTENTS OF YOUR GYM BAG

- Toiletry kit (a small case that includes a hairbrush/comb, deodorant, soap, shaving kit, shampoo/conditioner, toothbrush, toothpaste and dental floss,)
- Sturdy, "broken in" running shoes (no basketball or cross trainers, must be for jogging/running)
- Two casual civilian outfits (you will not be allowed to wear civilian clothes while in basic training, so don't bring anything expensive)
- Cotton white underwear (males get brown underwear issued, while females are given the chance to buy white cotton underwear at the reception station)
- Athletic supporters (males)/sports bras (females)-white only
- Female hygiene kit (females)
- Five pairs of white, calf length socks (no stripes or other markings)
- Towel and washcloth (No bright colors)
- ATM Card (occasionally you will be allowed to purchase items or services, so quick access to your money is essential)
- Sturdy watch (preferably waterproof, with alarm and nightlight)
- Pens/Pencil/Writing paper/Envelopes/Stamps/Small Notebook (You will need to take notes in class and you'll want to write home)
- Lock with Two Keys (Medium size. Drill sergeants keep one key in case you lose yours)
- Shower Shoes (Inexpensive flip-flops for walking around the barracks and in the shower)
- Small Ziploc Bags (to keep your notebook and papers dry)
- Portfolio or Large Envelope containing the following:
    - Marriage certificate
    - Divorce decrees (certified)
    - Birth certificates for children under 18 (certified)
    - Military orders sending you to training

- Enlistment contract
- Form SF 1199A & your bank account information (this will allow your paycheck to be electronically transferred. At BT, you will also be given the opportunity to open a bank account there.)
- Small address book with addresses and phone numbers of family, friends, your bank and other important contacts
- Your wallet should contain your social security card and your driver's license

WHAT NOT TO BRING

Now here's a list of things not to bring! The items not allowed are shipped home at your expense, thrown away, or locked away until graduation. So save yourself some time and effort, and do not bring them in the first place. Storage place is very limited! Your civilian bag and its contents will be inventoried during "shakedown" and then locked away until graduation. You see some interesting things during "shakedown" when trainees dump the contents of their bags on the ground. It's not unusual to see some of the things soldiers use as good luck charms or last-minute gifts from their loved ones. Don't bring these items:

- Large amounts of cash ($50-$75 is all you need. The only place to secure money will be in your wall locker.)
- Expensive jewelry (Do not wear more than your wedding band. Gold chains get lost. Remember, you'll have dogtags around your neck. Religious medallions are okay as long as they're sturdy and can be hidden under your t-shirt)
- Radios, CD Players, Walkmans, Boomboxes etc. (They'll get locked away along with your personal bag and civilian clothes. Even though these items are locked away, there's always a chance your stuff might turn up missing)
- Reading Material (You will not be allowed to read anything but

religious material. It's okay to bring magazines and books for your trip to basic training, but just be ready to pack these away in your civilian bag. Don't even attempt to bring pornographic or obscene material.)

- Perfume/Cologne (Drill Sergeants will not allow you to wear these. Save yourselves the hassle.)
- Alcohol, all tobacco products and chewing gum (They will all be confiscated. You can't smoke, drink or chew here. Some companies allow trainees to chew gum later in the cycle as a privilege. Most don't)
- Prescription medications not prescribed by a military physician
- Braces/Wraps for legs, knees or feet or asthma inhalers (A drill sergeant will send you to the troop medical clinic to be examined by a military physician to determine what you need. Nothing you received or were prescribed by a civilian doctor will be accepted for your use here)
- Robes/Negligees/Pajamas (You will sleep in your physical fitness uniform, which consists of a gray t-shirt and shorts. In cooler weather, you may wear the gray hooded sweatshirt and pants)
- Your family (You will see them at graduation)
- Your privately owned vehicle (Trainees are not authorized to drive personal vehicles while in basic training)
- Weapons (This includes small pocket knives)
- Make-up/Nail Polish (You will not be allowed to wear make-up during the daily training. Some companies allow female trainees to wear modest make-up at graduation)
- Toys/game devices/stuffed animals

CHAPTER 4.

ARRIVING AT YOUR BASIC TRAINING POST

You've been to the recruiting station and have asked extensive questions of your recruiter. Hopefully, he has shown you a few videos of what to expect in the Army. Don't believe that it's just like camping in your backyard! Don't laugh; there have been trainees who thought it would be like a camping trip. Do not allow yourself to be this naive. You've also picked a Military Occupational Specialty (MOS) depending on your aptitude, interests and Army needs. Hopefully, it's something you're interested in doing for the rest of your Army career. Do not let the recruiter pressure you! It is almost impossible to change your MOS after you arrive at basic training, SO BE SURE it's what you want and something you can live with! Read your contract carefully. It is binding. You really need to think about it for a few days and talk it over with family, especially your spouse, BEFORE YOU SIGN ANYTHING! Try to speak with soldiers who have recently completed basic training.

Even talking with veterans can be useful. If you haven't even gotten this far and are just curious, you can contact any local recruiter for information or check out some of the websites in the appendix. If you are looking for a recruiter locally, just look in your phone book, check out your library or ask your guidance counselor in school. You can even access the Army Recruiting website at http://www.goarmy.com and request that information be sent to you.

"I was born in Puerto Rico. I came to the Army to be somebody, to become a better human being. Basic Combat Training is very challenging, stressful and hard. I learned things and did things I would have never done as a civilian. I went through a lot of courses, fields and ranges. That taught me how to become a soldier."

YOUR FIRST DAYS AT THE RECEPTION STATION

When you say your tearful good-byes to your family and friends and board that plane or bus for the long journey into the unknown, you will be full of anxiety. This is perfectly normal and expected. Like most trainees, you will arrive at your basic training post late in the day, tired and irritable. Wear comfortable clothing and sensible shoes for your trip. Most trainees spend their first few days in-processing at a reception station or battalion before reporting to their basic training company. Depending on your arrival time, if late in the evening, you will probably be given a small snack. After you're briefed on the next day's events, which at this point have become a blur, you are finally allowed to go to sleep. Trainees are given a bunk and a wall locker in a large room with many other trainees of the same sex. Keep an eye on your things. Things have a tendency to disappear in these early hours when you're least aware. This is where that handy lock comes in if you brought it. Use it! If you arrive during the day, you might arrive just in time for a full hot meal. Afterwards, you might go into in-processing right away.

You'll spend about three to four days at the reception station or battalion. There will be non-commissioned officers (NCOs) ushering you around to all the different in-processing stations. You may think the stress level is high here, due to all the running around you must do and the anxiety associated with being away from home. Well, brace yourself. It is nothing compared to what happens upon arrival into your basic training company. Most reception stations also conduct a short version of the physical fitness test to separate those individuals sorely out of shape. These trainees are then placed in a Fitness Training Unit (FTU) before they ever arrive to their basic training unit! Depending on how out-of-shape you are, you could spend up to three weeks here in limbo!

"Reception and processing here is far different than what I went through when I joined the Air Force . . . Here we're held over for 4-5 days in what seems to be day camp. You get too relaxed in the fairly comfortable atmosphere at the 43rd (reception battalion) until you have to leave for your training company."

"The Reception Station was SO boring! In the civilian world, this in-processing would probably take two days at most–lots of 'hurry up and wait' here! We had an initial physical fitness (PT) test where we did a few push-ups, sit-ups and ran a mile. If we failed that, we were sent off to 'Fat Camp' before ever starting basic training!"

During in-processing at the reception station, the Army will start your financial and personnel records. You will get an Identification card and tags (dog tags). Representatives from local banks will give you the opportunity to open an account if you don't already have one. If you do not have the form SF 1199A, you will have to open an account with one of the local financial institutions. Twice a month, your pay will be electronically deposited into this account. You'll get an eye exam and be fitted for your first pair of glasses, if necessary. These military glasses look pretty gaudy and are affectionately called "birth control devices". You'll know what is meant by that when you see them.

You'll get the required immunization shots, an HIV test and a pregnancy test for females. Males will get their heads shaved and females will get the opportunity for a haircut. A bit of advice to females is to get a short haircut, as short as you can stand. If you insist on having long hair, you will always have to braid it. The standard for female hair is that it cannot hang below the bottom edge of your collar. This standard covers every uniform, including the physical fitness uniform. With all the rigorous training, by the end of the day, you'll resemble someone who has never seen a hairbrush. Your headgear may fit improperly and the constant pressure of a bun or braid on your head will give you a headache. Rest assured, long hair will grow back. Once you're out of basic training, you'll have more time for personal hygiene and styling your hair.

You will get your initial issue of military clothing here and start wearing your gray physical fitness uniform and camouflage Battle Dress Uniforms (BDUs) daily. Your initial issue consists of a duffel bag full of physical fitness uniforms, Battle Dress Uniforms (BDUs), boots (make sure they fit), t-shirts, socks and other items. You will be given an "advance pay". This "advance pay" is for you to buy necessities such as a shoe shine kit, washing detergent, towels, toiletry items, pens, note-books, etc. This means that your end of month paycheck will have a sizeable chunk taken out of it. So don't wonder what happened to all your money at the end of your first month in the Army. The reception station will give you a list of recommended items to buy at a mini-PX (Post Exchange), which is located at the reception station. Stick with the items on the list! Females are given a little more advance pay, because they have to buy specialty items such as white bras, pantyhose, a slip and white cotton panties. So, females, don't bother to bring colored underwear; the drill sergeants will make you pack it away. As you pull those leopard-skin bikinis out of your bag you could poten-tially become the center of unwanted attention. Don't splurge with this advance pay. Save it if you don't use it to buy all the recommended necessity items! Occasionally, you'll be allowed to make trips to the Post Exchange (PX) to restock your necessities.

Somewhere during this timeframe, a representative from your reception station will speak with you in a so-called "moment of truth" session. You are asked to speak honestly about any physical or mental problems you might have had in the past that would preclude you from finishing basic training. In some cases, trainees actively seek to hide or conceal the problem. In others, there is simply a failure to detect the problem at the Military Entrance Processing Station (MEPS). This can really seem impossible that these problems weren't detected earlier, but some trainees are either oblivious to what the Army's all about, or they tried to hide their problem from their recruiter. Imagine, the reception station at Ft Leonard Wood had a soldier report in without knee caps! For reasons unknown, this was not disclosed at the MEPS. He received a medical discharge, which was unfortunate. He could have saved himself some time and the Army some money had this been disclosed earlier.

The Army Is Not a Welfare Agency

PVT Smith was a quiet, reserved shy male. He usually followed orders well. Sometimes he would fly into a fit of rage and other times he would withdraw himself into a shell. After seeing a mental health counselor and psychiatrist, he was diagnosed with a severe mental condition and put on medication. He was immediately recommended for a medical discharge. On the day he was due to leave, he was given his civilian bag, which only had a trenchcoat, jeans and boots in it. The few other possessions he had owned, were thrown away at the reception station, earlier, deemed unfit to wear. He was quickly sent to the PX (Post Exchange) to buy a shirt. It turns out, this poor kid was homeless and without a family before he joined the Army. His home was a cardboard box under a bridge. He was only here for a warm meal and bed. It is difficult to send someone away in such a situation, but you have to understand that the Army is not a welfare agency. If you have a medical condition that was present before you entered the Army and it stops you from completing basic training, you will be discharged.

The "moment of truth" session is your chance to set the record straight. Be forthright and honest during this session. No one seeks to punish or penalize you for any disclosures. Just understand you are about to undergo the toughest and most intense challenge, both mentally and physically, you have likely ever faced. The last thing either you or the Army wants is to inadvertently cause you harm.

At this point, if the in-processing went smoothly and you didn't get stuck in a Fitness Training Unit (FTU), you are ready to go to your basic training company. During your stay at the reception station, you were only known as a roster number. You have probably made a few friends and are hoping that they are going to the same company as you. Chances are, they probably will.

YOUR FIRST DAY AT YOUR BASIC TRAINING COMPANY

Now the big day has arrived. A group of you is led to a holding area where you wait for "cattle trucks" to arrive. You will be sitting by your duffel bag and civilian bag, staring straight ahead. That's why it's so important you have only one light civilian bag with you. Your luggage will get very heavy, very quickly. Can you imagine being 4'11" and getting buried by your bags, because you fell down, only to be dug out by a drill sergeant?

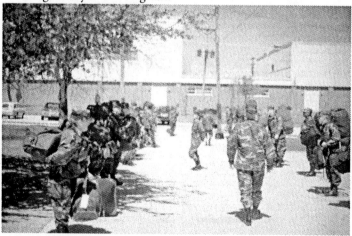

These soldiers are carrying the typical load of bags and are on their way to their basic training company.

Trainees are lined up one behind the other according to their roster number. You will sit quietly by your bags, while you wait for a drill sergeant or first sergeant, the senior ranking NCO, from the basic training company to come sign for you and the other trainees. Every trainee going to a basic training company must be accounted for. As you are signed for, you move together onto the "cattle trucks". You must carry both bags. It's a real balancing act, but can be done. Your drill sergeants make their first appearance at this pick-up. Usually, a group of them from the unit will stand and watch you board the truck. They won't however interfere with reception personnel, who are in charge of boarding. You'll be relaxed and thinking 'hey, this isn't all that bad, besides the drill sergeants seem pretty nice; they're all smiling'. Everything is orderly and not too rushed. It's truly the calm before the storm.

THE DREADED SHAKEDOWN

As soon as the "cattle trucks" arrive at your basic training company barracks, the drill sergeants are already waiting at the exit door of the truck. They greet you and your fellow trainees with a sharp torrent of orders. They want you, in no uncertain terms, to MOVE, MOVE, MOVE! Welcome to basic training, where you will indeed do more in a morning than most people do all day, just like the commercial says. This is now the start of your eight or nine weeks, which begins with a shakedown where all trainees are lined up and do everything in unison. The drill sergeants begin establishing themselves as authority figures right away. When they give an order, they expect an immediate and positive response.

Your next few hours are spent dumping personal and military articles on the floor and inventorying these items. Do these tasks quickly and efficiently unless you want to do push-ups, or other physical activity that will leave you totally exhausted by the end of the day.

Two trainees about to begin shakedown. They have just dumped the entire contents of all their bags on the ground. Each article will be inventoried and separated as needed.

"In the beginning, I didn't think or feel that I would make it through . . . One of the most vividly bad points during basic training was 'shakedown'. I was so scared during that time. I didn't know what to do—I was in shock. I felt, as if those drill sergeants were going to kill me. That was one of those times I didn't feel like I was going to make it."

After the shakedown, you will most likely be extremely tired and frightened. You will be divided into individual platoons and squads. You will be introduced to the individual drill sergeants of your platoon, take your bags to your bunks in your platoon area and be given an orientation. After each trainee is personally counseled by a drill sergeant on what is expected of him, given some basic rules and taught the platoon motto, he joins up with the rest of the company to go to the dining facility.

*"I'd like to pass on some words of advice! Never call a drill sergeant 'Sir' or 'Ma'am'! This will bring on a hailstorm of words directly 'in your face', as well as getting you 'dropped' for push-ups. They might even make a comment that **they** work for a living. Never 'eye-ball' a drill sergeant. This means don't ever stare them directly in the eye! If so, he's*

gonna eyeball you back . . . of course being 'in your face' again. Always be sure to answer a drill sergeant at the top of your lungs and end your response with a 'yes/no drill sergeant!' as they are notoriously hard of hearing."

COMPANY IN-PROCESSING AND THE FIRST DAYS OF TRAINING

More platoon and company in-processing continue throughout the next day before training ever starts. Trainees usually arrive at the reception station on a Monday, go to their basic training company on a Wednesday or Thursday and start their first official training day on Friday. Along with many orientation briefings, marching classes, and classes introducing the Army to you, a diagnostic physical fitness test will be given to you on Saturday.

Your first few days will be frustrating, while you figure out where everything is, the basic rules and what is expected of you. There's nothing more frightening than being sent on an errand and becoming lost. There will be a lot of standing and sitting around, while you wait to be counseled by your drill sergeants or while you fill out mountains of paperwork. You will sit through class after class, which come fast and furious, showing you everything from how to address your company commander to how to lace up your boots. You will find yourself wishing it was already Sunday, or worse yet, graduation day.

"When I first arrived at basic, I thought I had made a huge mistake. I just couldn't take all the yelling and the rushing around to do everything. I felt overwhelmed. If I didn't decide then and there to stick with it, I'd be the same person I was before basic—A person who was never able to finish anything where I might fail. I'm happy to say, I'm a better person for staying and have broken the vicious cycle of failure in my life."

"The classes were taught to help the slowest of people pass."

"The classroom material was long and tedious."

Chapter 5.

The Phases of Basic Training

The nine-week training cycle is divided into three phases, with distinct goals for each phase. Phase I, the most restrictive, lasts the first three weeks. Phase II, with more liberties and an increased focus on weapons training, takes place the next three weeks. Lastly, Phase III, where you start to hone your skills, covers the last three weeks.

Phase I–The Patriot Phase (Weeks 1-3)

In Phase I, you are under total control of the drill sergeants with little or no free time. Drill sergeants monitor everything you do. You are introduced to the buddy system. As mentioned before, the buddy system involves assigning a "buddy" of the same sex to each soldier. This is your battle buddy. Throughout training, you assist and support each other. Now is also the time the soldierization process is begun. This is merely the process by which the Army turns you from a civilian into a well-disciplined, physically and mentally fit soldier. This is rough for a lot of people, because it frequently involves doing something you don't feel like doing or are afraid of doing.

The first three weeks of basic training creates the most stress and uncertainty in each trainee. Imagine bringing together about 150-250 people from all different walks of life and backgrounds to work and live together in one set of barracks. Trainees each cycle, consistently fall into three major categories. In the first category, always the largest, are people willing to go along with everything, having a genuine interest in doing whatever it takes to succeed. In the second category, are those few consistently rebelling against everything that is expected of them as well as to all authority figures, especially the drill sergeants. The third category consists of a few people who are withdrawn, unable to adjust socially and mentally to the military environment, though they try to fit in initially. The latter are usually loners, whose problems don't surface until the third or fourth week of training. Throughout the training cycle, trainees may fluctuate among the three categories.

The goals for soldiers in Phase I include: learning the importance of paying attention to detail, learning to conform to basic Army standards and customs (for example, there are certain ways you stand in formation, talk to an officer and make your bunks), mastering basic skills (including classes in Army communications and first aid), maintaining yourself and your platoon area, and developing your physical fitness to a higher level.

"In my life, I have done a lot of things. I have had parties, fun and acted as if it wasn't wrong. Basic training for me was discipline. My drill instructors molded me from a punk to a man. I hated getting up so early. We couldn't drink soda pop, and I was homesick."

DRILL SERGEANTS— "WHO IS THIS PERSON ANYWAY?"

Okay, so what does all that mean? In Phase I, trainees are continuously guided by their drill sergeants. This means that you don't make a lot of decisions on your own. The drill sergeants make them for you. You will always recognize a basic training company in Phase I as they march by. Not only will they be marching out of step and look somewhat confused, but there will be one private carrying a red guidon (flag) in the front of the formation, letting everyone know that this is a Phase I company. A basic training battalion has four to five companies with about 1000 trainees in varying stages of training. Each company runs its own daily training. A company consists of four platoons of trainees. Each platoon in a company has about 30-55 trainees, run by a platoon sergeant (also a drill sergeant), and two to three additional drill sergeants. If the unit is "gender-integrated" and has males and females, then there must be one female drill sergeant assigned to each platoon. These drill sergeants are the "cream of the crop" of the Army. Drill sergeant candidates are selected by the Department of the Army or are volunteers. After graduating a two-month long rigorous Drill Sergeant School, they do a two or three year tour of duty as a drill sergeant. Most drill sergeants have been in the Army about 10-15 years. They have a wealth of experience and different types of assignments behind them. Not all are infantry soldiers; some come from other Army branches (ie Engineers, Transportation, Medical, Chemical). Of course, the posts that only train infantry (Combat Arms) soldiers have only infantry or combat arms drill sergeants. The Combat Arms (CA) branches include Infantry, Armor, Artillery, Aviation and Engineers. For posts such as Ft Leonard Wood and Ft Jackson, where combat support and combat service support MOSs are trained, there is a mixture of drill sergeants from different branches, including Infantry. Combat

Support (CS) and Combat Service Support (CSS) branches include all Army personnel who support the Combat Arms, such as administration, medical, logistics, food services, legal, finance and transportation.

"The drill sergeants are very stressful. I guess that's their job. They work with your mind to see how much you can take. They work your body so you could become physically ready."

"My drill sergeants were very helpful. They were willing to help each and every soldier. That's one thing I really liked."

"My drill sergeants at first seemed to be crazy animals whose sole objective was to scream and make us look like idiots, they still do, though I'm no longer terrified of them, because I know what is going on. None of them beat me up or anything so I've got nothing to complain about."

"The sergeants came in all shapes and sizes and the mix per platoon was excellent. I rarely felt as though I couldn't talk to one of them."

It is easy to point out a unit that is in Phase I of training. Trainees fight with each other on a regular basis, mostly verbal although sometimes physical. You will get little sleep and will be constantly stressed. You will resist working together and become constantly frustrated. Frequently, there is tension between the sexes and soldiers who have never worked with others from different backgrounds and races. You probably won't be accustomed to getting up so early. You have only 20-30 minutes to get dressed and cleaned up in the morning, fighting for space in front of a sink. Doing physical training everyday with sore muscles and constantly learning new things both become a real challenge. Most trainees are homesick, miss their families and think they've made a mistake, coming into the Army.

The Uncooperative Private

Several trainees complained about a fellow soldier to their drill sergeant. He never wanted to do his share in the morning, and his buddies finally got tired of it. When a drill sergeant spoke with the trainee about his behavior, he shrugged it off, saying he liked to do things his way. This trainee did very well in the physical training sessions, probably the top athlete in the company, but he didn't like working together. He felt he could do it on his own and that he was doing well. He constantly had to be counseled by the drill sergeants and was in danger of being kicked out of the Army. In the fourth week, he was a different person. He was frantic. Why? He could not grasp the concepts of firing the M16A2 Rifle, a requirement for graduation. Drill sergeants spent additional hours retraining him and suggested that in his off-time he get together with other soldiers who were doing well. Because of his earlier behavior, he found this extremely difficult and really sweated it out on the rifle qualification ranges.

Don't get an attitude if you feel you are better than everyone else. Chances are, you won't be the best in everything and might even need someone else's help somewhere down the road. Keep your options open. Help others, and they will help you. Cooperate and others will cooperate with you.

Listed below are the classes traditionally taught in the first three weeks (these classes are explained in detail in the glossary):

Alcohol & Drug Prevention

Army Values

Basic Military Communications

Code of Conduct

Conduct an Army Physical Fitness Session

Drill and Ceremonies

Environmental Awareness

Equal Opportunity

First Aid Classes

Guard Duty Classes

Heritage & Traditions

Healthy Lifestyles

Identification & Wear of Uniforms

Introduction to a Physical Fitness Program

Law of Land Warfare

Military Customs & Courtesies

Military Justice

Map Reading

Nuclear, Biological and Chemical (NBC) Defense
Personal Health & Hygiene
Sabotage & Espionage Directed Against the US Army (SAEDA)
Safety
Standards of Ethical Conduct
Terrorism/Threat Orientation
Unexploded Ordnance Briefing
A typical day in Phase I starts with waking up (First Call) at 4:00 am (0400 hrs). The first formation is at 4:30 am in the Army physical fitness uniform (gray t-shirt and shorts with gray sweatshirt and sweatpants, depending on the weather). You will conduct physical fitness training almost every day. A roll call is taken first to account for everyone.

GOING ON SICKCALL

Sickcall is the time set aside for you to go the troop medical clinic for diagnosis and treatment of an illness or injury. Trainees going on sickcall are separated from the rest of the company. They usually report to first formation in the work uniform, the BDU—Battle Dress Uniform. You should only go on sickcall when you feel you have an injury or are ill. Drill sergeants cannot stop you from going on sickcall. It's your right. It's every soldier's right. Of course, every cycle there are trainees who abuse this right and miss too much training, which can cause them to be "new started" into another unit. Being "new started" is the just the process applied to someone who has missed too much training and must start over in another training company.

Going on sickcall, is like trying to leave the stadium after a ballgame, especially if you go on a Monday. Sickcall is not available on Sunday, unless you have a real emergency. When you go, expect the medical facility to be packed full of trainees. The earlier you arrive, the faster you will be seen and the faster you can return to training. Frequently, some soldiers like to go to sickcall and sit around to keep from going to training. Don't fall into this group of slackers! That is why it is so crowded! All the training you miss, will only get you "new started" into another company, which will only delay your graduation from basic training. Who wants to be in basic training longer than they have to?

If you are truly sick or injured, bear with the health care professionals. They try to run the show as efficiently as possible. Tell them exactly what symptoms you are experiencing. If your problem is minor, such as a cold or flu, you will probably receive medications and possibly a code. If you have some kind of injury that needs rest, you will most definitely receive a code. Many trainees are angry when they receive a code, but it is in their best interest to follow the recommendations of the doctor. If you try to disregard the code, you might end up being out of commission longer than you originally thought. This can sometimes turn out to be a vicious cycle of going on and off code.

THE DAILY PHYSICAL FITNESS SESSION

After roll call and the separation of the sick call soldiers, the remainder of the company begins physical fitness training. Most units alternate, doing muscular strength and endurance training on one day (mostly push-ups and sit-ups), then a cardio-respiratory activity, usually "ability group runs" (AGRs) the other day. Ability group runs are conducted with other soldiers in the company, who run at a similar pace to you. After every physical fitness test, trainees are re-divided into running groups. Muscular strength and endurance training is done mostly on a platoon level, although sometimes you will train with the entire company. The company may be split up into three or four different running groups, with the slowest group always being the largest initially. This is because more and more people show up for basic training being totally out of shape. Occasionally, you may run as a whole company to build team spirit and morale.

"No matter how fast you run or how high you jump, your drill sergeant will always tell you that his grandmother does it better. Yeah, yeah, now what kind of person would have a grandmother like that?."

THE DIAGNOSTIC BASIC PHYSICAL FITNESS TEST

Within the first few days at your training company, you will take part in a diagnostic physical fitness test. The drill sergeants use the results of this test to develop a physical fitness plan for your level of physical fitness. The test consists of doing push-ups, sit-ups and a two-mile run. The push-up is the first event. You are given two minutes to do as many correct push-ups as you can. After a chance to rest for a few minutes, you have two minutes to do the sit-ups. To increase the challenge and stress on your body in this test, the two-mile run is conducted after the push-ups and sit-ups. The two mile run is either conducted on a ¼-mile track (eight laps = two miles) or on a straightaway (one mile each way). At the end of the test, your points are added and you are given a total score. If your total score is less than 90 points, consider yourself out of shape.

The results of the diagnostic physical fitness test are generally very low. It is not unusual to see trainees unable to complete even one push-up or sit-up. More often than not, some females have considerable difficulty holding up their body weight during the push-up, due to weaker upper body strength. A small percentage of males and females have weak abdominal strength and strain, unable to pull their bodies up during the sit-up. Many trainees walk most of the two mile run. If you are in poor physical shape, you may take anywhere from 20-30 minutes to finish the run. Do not be alarmed with these low scores, but do realize that you have only eight or nine weeks to improve your score. Most basic training posts have what are called Fitness Training Units (FTUs) to bring those trainees who need it, up to a marginal level of fitness before even starting basic training. Remember that every physical fitness session counts towards improving your physical conditioning and your score! Be ready to take a physical fitness test every two weeks. Your scores should steadily be increasing. Your goals should include improving your physical fitness level and achieving 50 points in every event.

TRAINEE LEADERSHIP POSITIONS AND PREPARING FOR TRAINING

After the hour-long physical fitness session, you have 20-30 minutes to shower and change into your BDUs. Part of this time is allocated for you to organize your personal and common barracks areas. The drill sergeants closely monitor this during Phase I. Some trainees still have difficulty making their bunks correctly. Footwear must be aligned properly under your bunks. You will be assigned a wall locker to store all your gear. Each wall locker must look exactly the same, on the inside, as well as the outside.

Training schedules are posted in the barracks. The drill sergeants will assign a platoon guide trainee to each platoon. This guide may be you or another trainee who shows leadership ability and the motivation to do well. Each squad in a platoon, with 7-15 trainees per squad, is assigned a trainee squad leader, who assists the platoon guide. These leadership positions are rotated throughout the cycle. Some platoons average about four platoon guides per cycle. There may be as many as eight different guides in a cycle. The trainee leaders assist the platoon sergeant in keeping accountability of trainees, as well as in relaying information from the drill sergeants to the trainees. Usually the night before training, the drill sergeant will brief the platoon guide on the next day's activities, formation times and the uniform. Platoon guides and squad leaders are still treated the same as the other privates in the platoon and do not have any types of special privileges.

After trainees finish getting ready and are in the proper uniform, they run outside to formation. You are encouraged to run everywhere. The drill sergeants say that if you are walking, you are wrong. They tend to zero-in on trainees not moving quickly enough. On certain scheduled days before breakfast, you will turn in your used bed linen and receive a clean set. A few times a week, you will also have Quartermaster laundry turn-in to turn in your dirty uniforms. Then after everyone is accounted for, you will be marched to chow for breakfast.

EATING IN
THE DINING FACILITY

Most of your meals will be in the dining facility. This was called the mess hall in the old days. This facility is a cafeteria-style setting where all the soldiers in the battalion take their meals. Companies are rotated through the chow line every 15 minutes for each meal. So you may have more than one company eating at the dining facility with overlapping times. Your first meal of the day, breakfast in the Army, is still as hearty as it has always been. Most big eaters will be happy to know that the dining facility still serves the basics: sausage, bacon, grits, eggs and potatoes. In addition you will most likely have a choice of French toast, pancakes or waffles. Sometimes you'll see oatmeal and various hot fruit toppings for the pancakes and waffles. There is a fruit bar that includes cold cereal and yogurt, plus juice, milk and water. The entire company has only 40 minutes to rotate through the dining facility. This gives you, the individual about 15-20 minutes to eat. You must eat fairly quickly and without talking to other trainees.

After the morning's training, you march back to the dining facility for lunch. Lunch is 40 minutes long also and starts anywhere from 1130 hours to 1300 hours (1:00 PM). Lunch has three meat choices, a choice of starch (such as rice or potatoes), a choice of two vegetables, a choice of dessert, and a large salad and fruit bar. Again, the same rules for breakfast are enforced here. While standing in the chow line, you stand at the position of parade rest, with your feet shoulder width apart and arms crossed behind your back. Next, you shout out your social security number, so the food service worker or drill sergeant monitoring the beginning of the line can write it down. Lastly, you sign your name on the food service roster next to your social security number before grabbing your tray.

After lunch the company marches back to training. Once training is done, you march back to the dining facility for dinner. It sure seems like you eat often here, but once you start the rigorous training, you'll be hungry all the time and looking forward to the meals. Dinner is 40 minutes and is similar to lunch.

"The food has been above average. I like the idea that there are salad bars and they are well stocked. Why does the Army serve so many potatoes?"

YOUR FIRST DAY OF CLASSES

After breakfast, you march to your first period of instruction or class. The distances are mostly less than a mile. You won't carry a lot of gear the first few days. You'll wear a soft cap, rather than the much heavier Kevlar helmet initially. During Phase I, drill and ceremonies and classroom type classes are the norm, most of which are indoors. Because of high stress levels, many trainees have trouble sleeping at night, and you'll struggle to stay awake and alert in class. Of course, drill sergeants keep a sharp watch and anyone caught sleeping or drifting off is pulled to the back of the class to exercise. The best way to fight the "sleep monster" is to try to eat well, get some sleep at night and drink lots of water to keep from feeling lethargic. This is also where the buddy system comes in—keep your buddy awake! If the guy next to you is falling asleep, give him a jab.

"Phase I dealt mostly with classes and learning customs and courtesies. It was hard to stay awake at times, but you better believe I kept those eyes OPEN!"

After dinner, drill sergeants conduct reinforcement training (reinforce the tasks the soldiers learned) and make-up training for soldiers who missed training, such as soldiers who were on sickcall that morning.

THE GAS CHAMBER

Talk to any recent graduate of basic training, and they will almost inevitably mention the gas chamber. Imagine standing in a room with concentrated smoke (CS) floating in the air around you. Imagine knowing that you will have to inhale some of this CS after you remove your mask, which is quite a bit stronger than tear gas. Some privates try to hold their breath and to close their eyes. Unfortunately, the drill sergeants can see this right away and usually make the private speak a few words. If you want to take in as little gas as you can, you can try taking a deep breath before you take your mask off, keep your eyes open and then try to hold your breath without looking obvious. If all else fails, just take in small breaths and then let it all drool out when you exit the chamber. Take comfort in the fact that every soldier in today's Army went through the chamber, including your drill sergeants. No one is immune to this stuff when they breathe it in! You will survive too and you will laugh about it later.

THIE

Before you even journey into the chamber, you are given an extensive class on nuclear, chemical and biological warfare. You learn how to assemble, disassemble and care for your protective mask and clothing. You are given detailed instructions on what to do and what to expect in the chamber. Most trainees are frightened to death before this event, but the only way to really gain confidence in your mask, is to see if it really works. That's the whole purpose behind going through the gas chamber.

Soldiers ready to unmask inside the gas chamber. Notice the fine haze of CS gas in the air.

"The gas chamber was a horrible experience. I thought that I was going to die. I didn't feel that they would open the door soon enough to let me out. I felt like I was being tortured. I couldn't breathe, I couldn't see—all I knew was everything was burning."

DISCIPLINARY PROBLEMS

You might be wondering how the drill sergeants and other cadre deal with disciplinary problems during these first stressful weeks. You might even have visions of a trainee being beaten up by a drill sergeant. Well, today's Army is much different than what you see on television or in the movies. Drill sergeants and cadre can only touch you for safety reasons, or as an instructional tool. If you are falling off an obstacle or a drill sergeant wants to correct your hand position in the salute, he is then authorized to touch you.

Initially, when soldiers commit minor infractions, drill sergeants deal with these infractions on their level by stern words and extra physical training (for example, push-ups). They also use "group discipline" techniques to try to motivate that individual. For example, if a soldier isn't following along, a drill sergeant may make the entire group do physical training for that one soldier's actions. In other words, peer pressure works pretty well here. This type of corrective discipline is used extensively in the first few weeks, but as training progresses, you are held more and more responsible for your own actions.

"What I liked about basic were the discipline building techniques and motivational techniques used by my drill sergeants. Before I came to basic, I was a chronic procrastinator, and since I've been here, I've managed to begin my task either earlier in the morning or prepare myself at night. Motivation was part of my problem also, but as you already know, motivation provided by the drill sergeants could jump start the worst kind of procrastinator."

The final level of handling disciplinary problems is with the company commander and first sergeant. The company commander is the officer in charge of the company in the rank of captain. The first sergeant is the senior non-commissioned officer (NCO) in the company. He is the master trainer, senior advisor to the commander and oversees all the drill sergeants.

THIE

THE UNIFORM CODE OF MILITARY JUSTICE (UCMJ) AND THE ARTICLE 15

The Uniform Code of Military Justice (UCMJ) is the foundation of the Military Justice System. It is a Federal Statute, which governs all the Armed Services (Army, Navy, Air Force, Marines and Coast Guard). As in the civilian world, commanders and their subordinates see a broad spectrum of misconduct. At the most serious end are crimes similar to civilian society (such as murder, rape and grand theft), known in the military as serious offenses. Less serious civilian and military offenses are known as minor offenses (such as destruction of property and disturbing the peace). Below these, are even less significant acts of misconduct which have no real counterpart in the civilian world known as minor infractions. These may include: failing to obey an order, making a false official statement, Absent Without Leave (AWOL) and disrespect towards an NCO or officer. These minor infractions are the most frequent types of offenses you will see in basic training.

To maintain discipline and good order, commanders are authorized under what's known as the Article 15 of the UCMJ, to administer punishment for these minor types of infractions. Every commander in the Army has the right to impose this type of non-judicial punishment. It's called non-judicial, because there is no judge involved. For these types of minor infractions, a commander will choose to have a soldier report to him for an Article 15 proceeding. The commander will read the infraction the soldier was alleged to have made and give him the opportunity to accept Article 15 proceedings or to choose a courts-martial.

It is every soldier's right to choose a courts-martial, but rarely does anyone choose it. The stakes are much higher at the courts-martial level. Usually, once the soldier finds out the highest punishment they could receive if convicted in a courts-martial, they listen more closely to the proceedings and inevitably choose the Article 15 for these minor infractions. Some courts-martial offenses can carry considerable jail time, reduction in rank and dishonorable discharges from the Army if convicted. After the trainee chooses to continue with the Article 15 proceeding, the soldier is given the opportunity to seek legal advice and then reports back to the commander. The Article 15 proceeding is like a "mini-court". The commander acts as the judge and jury, reading any sworn statements by witnesses and listening to any testimony from witnesses and/or the soldier. The commander then has to make a decision if the soldier is guilty. If the soldier is found not guilty, the soldier is released and no punishment is given. If guilty, the commander then gives the trainee his punishment. Punishment can consist of restriction (no free time), extra duty (working after the duty day when everyone else is released for free time) and/or money taken out of the soldier's pay.

It is difficult for a commander to say beforehand what will make him initiate an Article 15 proceeding. Commanders have to look at a variety of different factors in each case. Each commander strives to maintain good order and discipline and uses the Article 15 as a tool to achieve these. Here are some examples of when a trainee may receive punishment under an Article 15 proceeding: a soldier who used a curse word with a drill sergeant, a soldier who ran away (AWOL), two soldiers who were found having sexual intercourse, a soldier who consistently threatened others or a soldier who would not obey an order. Most of the time, if a trainee turns himself around, these Article 15s will not follow him to his next assignment and will not appear anywhere on his military records. Otherwise, they could come back to haunt him.

An Article 15 Turned This Private Around

PVT Carrington always had to do something opposite from what he was supposed to do. He followed orders unwillingly and when he did follow orders, he made it known that he didn't like it. He kept telling everyone who would listen, that he didn't want to be in the Army,

THIE

because he just couldn't take orders from anyone. In almost every class, he would miss a large portion of the instruction, because he was out on the grass doing additional motivational 'training' with the drill sergeants. He would come back into the classroom, dirty, sweaty and out of breath. This usually moves a soldier to follow orders but not PVT Carrington. The next step, if the drill sergeants are having no luck, is to see the first sergeant and the commander. The soldier ended up receiving non-judicial punishment (Article 15) from the commander, which really woke him up. He had a family at home that was counting on his paycheck, and he realized how stupid he was to risk his new career. Afterwards, he became one of the better soldiers, even doing well in a squad leader position.

Sometimes, it is the case where a trainee cannot be turned around. Some trainees receive additional training from the drill sergeants and numerous Article 15s from the commander and still cannot follow orders or work as part of a group. After these soldiers have been counseled by the chaplain, mental health professionals, reserve/national guard liaison personnel (if applicable), their platoon sergeant, first sergeant and commander, they are discharged from the Army. They are usually given an Entry Level Separation (ELS) discharge (explained in Chapter 9) for their failure to adapt to the Army. The Army makes every effort to help a trainee before it gets this far, but occasionally, even the Army can't help this kind of individual. Not everyone is able to adapt to a military environment, and the Army is not meant for everyone.

Phase II–The Gunfighter Phase (White)

Phase II starts at the beginning of the fourth week of training and continues through the sixth week. The ceremony to switch your red guidon with a white one is one of real fanfare! The drill sergeants slowly lessen the total control; trainees are given a little more free time and are expected to perform some tasks on their own, with little guidance. The focus here is to develop individual soldier skills and trainee leaders. You will begin to work as a team and develop self-discipline.

"During Phase II, you could see the transitioning among the soldiers. We were slowly becoming soldiers rather than civilians in BDUs."

Some of the classes typically taught in Phase II are:
Basic Rifle Marksmanship
Fire and Maneuver Course
Hand Grenade Range
Hand to Hand Combat Training
Individual Tactical Training
Rifle Bayonet Training
US Weapons

A TYPICAL PHYSICAL FITNESS SESSION IN PHASE II

Most trainees start getting adjusted to military life by the fourth week. A typical day might begin at 4:00 am with First Call. Since you sleep in your physical fitness uniform, it's just a matter of making a quick trip to the latrine before you go outside for formation. Some basic training posts allow you to purchase gray spandex to wear underneath your shorts. If you wear these, make sure not to sleep in them! They will hold in too much moisture throughout the night and increase your chances of rashes and infection.

By 4:30 am, you start the physical fitness session. If it's a running day, you are split up into your running groups, stretch for a few minutes and then off you go. Depending on what group you're in, you could run anywhere from two to five miles on the average. Trainees lagging behind on the run are pushed even harder by the drill sergeants. The front of the running group frequently turns around to pick up the stragglers left behind. Of course, this makes the distance the group runs much longer than the distance the stragglers run. This is an effective way of using peer pressure. Some privates are tempted to try to always link up with the slow group. Don't let this happen to you! Drill sergeants will eventually know you're in the wrong group, and if you're not pushing yourself enough, your fitness level will not improve, and you will not pass the physical fitness test.

After returning to the barracks area, you spend a few more minutes stretching, checking your heart rate and are released to clean up. Once you return to the barracks you have about 30 minutes, if you're lucky, to change into your BDUs and then march off to breakfast. If you are running with the slowest ability group, you often are the last group to come in and have less time to change. This can be an incentive to push yourself to move up to a faster running group. As mentioned earlier, after each new physical fitness test, the groups are divided again to reflect the new running times from the test.

On days where you concentrate on muscular strength and endurance, the platoon remains together or the company might train as a whole. There are a variety of different exercises to improve your strength, but inevitably, you'll be doing many different variations of push-ups and sit-ups. You will really be getting down and dirty, rolling back and forth on the ground. Sometimes, you may get lucky if your company has mats, but more than likely you'll be in the grass or sawdust. There's nothing more uncomfortable than picking sawdust out of your shorts, but it soon becomes routine.

A DAY OUT ON THE RANGES

During Phase II, most of the day is spent out on ranges. Most of these training sites are away from the barracks and consist of weapons firing and proficiency training. It's more hectic on days when you go to ranges, because you must make an extra trip to the arms room. This is a secure place where your weapon is stored. Throughout basic training, you will have an M16A2 rifle assigned to you and you only. A few three to eight kilometer footmarches are incorporated during this phase. In the summer, you march out to the range, when it's cooler. In the winter, you'll march back at the end of the day. All other transportation is by "cattle truck". Once at the range, you are given an orientation, a class and a safety briefing.

This soldier is watching for his targets downrange during a practice session on the rifle qualification course. The drill sergeants can assist during this practice phase, pointing out targets and watching your form. On the day of the real qualification, you're completely on your own!

"I loved firing the rifle and the machine gun! I wish I had had more time to learn everything, because I felt like I was rushed through."

"Basic Rifle Marksmanship was good, it goes by quick and it's good the way it is taught."

Since you are a considerable distance from the dining facility, lunch is brought to you. This is known as Field Chow. The hot food is brought out to the site in insulated containers and a serving line is set up. There are two meat choices included and the desserts are either fruit or pre-packaged cakes or pies. In the summer, when you need to be at a range very early to beat the heat, you may also have field chow for breakfast, which includes the usual offerings from the dining facility, although the eggs tend to be a bit runny.

After lunch, it's back to training. Whenever training runs behind or if you have a larger than normal company, the range may continue running through lunch as soldiers are rotated through the chow line. By the end of the day, you're either dead tired from the heat or dead tired from freezing the whole day and are ready to get back. Again, with large companies, dinner might be field chow, otherwise it's dinner in the dining facility. In the evenings, drill sergeants still conduct some type of reinforcement training. Although, with some of these ranges, it is too difficult to make-up the training immediately and another time has to be scheduled for those who missed it.

BEING ON FIREGUARD

In the evening, when drill sergeants leave for the night, one drill sergeant remains at the barracks on duty. He is known as the charge of quarters (CQ). Each floor in the barracks has a requirement to provide two trainees every hour to patrol the halls. All trainees in the company are rotated through these positions. These soldiers are known as fireguards. They were originally established years ago to act as a fire watch in the old wooden barracks troops used to live in. Today, it is more a test of self-discipline. Can these two trainees stay awake their entire shift? It's not uncommon to see a trainee, fast asleep, leaning against a wall. By order of the charge of quarters, he could spend the rest of his shift patrolling the halls wearing his rucksack and Kevlar helmet. More importantly though, the fireguards check to ensure there is no interaction between the sexes or intruders in the barracks. During their shift, they report directly to the charge of quarters, who also makes his own rounds. Don't be surprised if you see a drill sergeant walking around in his socks, so as not to announce his presence.

Tearing Paper Into Strips

In D Company, a fireguard once found a PVT Sterling in the latrine, tearing paper into little strips. After the commander spoke with the trainee, he immediately called a mental health counselor to talk to the private. The commander discovered later, that the soldier was a schizophrenic and had the fireguard not found him, he might have hurt himself or someone else. He had been a model soldier up to this point, and something in him just seemed to snap. As mentioned earlier, the Army does not provide long term treatment for soldiers with mental problems and the soldier had to be discharged.

Phase III– The Warrior Phase (Blue)

Phase III begins at the start of the seventh week and continues through the end of the ninth week of training. You now have a blue guidon. The trainees are expected to accomplish most tasks on their own without any supervision. They exercise a greater amount of self-discipline and do what's right, even when no one is watching. The culmination of this phase is a field training exercise, where soldiers are able to practice the skills they learned as well as giving them an opportunity to lead their fellow trainees. Two major events in this phase include the final Basic Physical Fitness Test and the "hands-on" End-of-Cycle Test (EOCT). This EOCT is a test where you are graded on your ability to perform a variety of tasks, rather than a written examination.

"The one thing I didn't expect was how much studying I had to do for the End of Cycle Test and the final inspection."

Since most of the classroom type classes are taught in the beginning of basic training, most of the training in the third phase is conducted outside and on ranges in all types of weather. Some ranges are even conducted at night. The days really seem to drag on!

"The night fire ranges gave a realistic idea of how war could be if I ever had to go."

Listed below are the typical ranges and classes you might encounter:

Army Family Teambuilding Class
Conditioning Obstacle Course (PECS)
Confidence Obstacle Course
Day and Night Defensive Firing
End of Cycle Test
Field Training Exercise (FTX)

Night Infiltration Course/Night Offensive Firing

Reinforcement Training in preparation for the End-of-Cycle Test (EOCT)

A day in Phase III is similar to a day in Phase II, except trainees may be given more free time in the evening when there are no night ranges scheduled. They might even be allowed to buy sodas and candy at the "mini-PX" at the end of the day. The focus now is on reinforcing the skills you learned at the beginning of basic training, so you will do well on the End-of-Cycle Test and hopefully carry your knowledge with you to Advanced Individual Training (AIT) and beyond. AIT is your next stop after basic training, where you learn the skills of your particular MOS.

At this point, final preparations are made to improve your physical fitness level. This is your last chance to pass the Basic Physical Fitness Test before graduation. If you are unable to pass the test, you will not graduate on time with your company.

Stay True to Yourself

PVT Chi was from Hawaii, a little chubby and had to work harder than others on his physical fitness. He was moderately overweight when he arrived and had trouble keeping up on runs. Even though he made great strides in improving his running ability, he wasn't able to pass the two-mile run on the final fitness test. Instead of telling his parents not to come, he pretended to call them to inform them he wouldn't be graduating. It must have been extremely embarrassing for his parents who showed up on graduation day, to not see their son graduate. Instead, PVT Chi worked in the kitchen in the dining facility. Luckily, this story does have a happy ending. A week later, PVT Chi passed his physical fitness test, and was able to move on to his AIT. Unfortunately, the friends he had made in basic training were in the class ahead of him.

Trainees are given an additional two weeks after graduation to pass the physical fitness test, and if there are no extenuating circumstances, and they still fail, they will most likely be discharged from the Army. If you fail the End-of-Cycle Test, you will be given another chance to pass.

THE FIELD TRAINING EXERCISE

Towards the end of the cycle, the company goes out on a field training exercise. You'll pitch your pup tent, camouflage yourself and learn to live out in the woods. All meals are either field chows or Meals-Ready-To-Eat (MREs). These meals are pre-packaged, vacuum-sealed or freeze dried food packets. The novelty of these MREs quickly wears off after you have eaten a few of them. For some reason, many trainees say they tend to make you pretty constipated.

Out in the field, as it's called, you'll go out on patrols in the daytime, as well as at night. The drill sergeants may have teamwork reaction courses set up to test how the members of your squad and platoon work together as a unit. This is a tactical environment, where you will use blank ammunition and drill sergeants use artillery, grenade, smoke and concentrated smoke (CS) simulators to simulate a realistic combat environment. All these simulators are known as pyrotechnics. This Field Training Exercise (FTX) lasts three or four days. Some companies like to take their trainees out for one overnight or more, earlier in the cycle in a non-tactical environment to practice setting up a pup tent and sleeping in one. This is called Bivouac and is conducted in a non-tactical environment. There are no pyrotechnics used as the focus is on learning to adapt to surviving outdoors. For someone who has never slept on the ground and in the dirt, this can be pretty traumatic.

The Field Training Exercise (FTX) is your last big training event, although some companies like to plan the End-of-Cycle Test (EOCT) as the culminating event. Observing privates at the field site, it's astounding to see how far the trainees have come. It truly gives you a sense of accomplishment to see that shy trainee, giving orders and leading his squad through the woods on an ambush patrol or that one trainee finally able to keep up on a roadmarch. The trainees are on a real high, feeling as if they can conquer anything. The drill sergeants are tired, but wouldn't trade places with anyone in the world. Of course, they also look forward to cycle break, when they will have a break from training privates. This time in between cycles is used to give drill sergeants some free time and to work on developing their own skills.

"Never walk around without your chinstrap fastened! My drill sergeant saw me run by in the field and ordered me to stand in front of him. I knew immediately what was wrong! He asked me if I knew what Kevlar artillery was. Of course I didn't know and he responded by tearing my helmet off and throwing it down the embankment. Of course my battle buddy and I spent the next ten minutes combing the underbrush for it. When I got back the whole squad was being 'dropped' and boy did I feel like an idiot."

GRADUATION WEEK

Believe it or not, this is probably the most hectic week of basic training. You will spend long hours cleaning gear and your weapon, getting final uniform fittings, cleaning the barracks, finishing up any make-up training, going through graduation rehearsals and working to pass your physical fitness test or End-of-Cycle Test if you failed the first time.

Companies traditionally conduct their final physical fitness test and the End-of-Cycle Test (EOCT) before the Field Training Exercise (FTX). This leaves that last week to tie up all the loose ends and retest the failures. Apprehension will start to surface as you start thinking about your Advanced Individual Training (AIT), especially if you will be travelling to a different post. If you have family coming, you'll be excited about that too.

You'll be spending most of your free time cleaning your gear and your weapon before you turn them in. Not only will your gear and weapon be scrutinized during various inspections this week, but you will also be tested on your soldier knowledge. You will wear your dress green uniform (Class A) during these inspections. It's not rare for you to clam up under the pressure to answer a question from the battalion commander, who could be standing right in front of you.

Most training posts conduct some type of graduation activities that family, friends and trainees can participate in together. These activities usually start the day before graduation. You will be given the option to take your family to a banquet or maybe a picnic in the summer. They'll get a chance to eat in your dining facility. Or maybe, you'll have a big craving to eat "fast food" and skip the festivities all together. There will also be plenty of briefings for your families if they are interested in attending.

Depending on the schedules of the other companies in your battalion, you may graduate with just your company or the whole battalion. Some battalions, in warmer weather, like to conduct large-scale graduations on parade fields with a lot of marching and hoopla. Others prefer the comfort of a theater or other indoor arena, to show videos and slides. It is really up to the individual company, how they want to conduct their graduation.

After the graduation ceremony or the family lunch in the dining facility, there is a flurry of activity as you are separated into groups. If you will be conducting your Advanced Individual Training (AIT) at the same post as your basic training, you will leave that day to go to your new AIT company. Frequently, these companies give you the weekend off to spend with your family before training starts. If you are travelling by bus or plane to your new AIT post, you may leave that day, or sometime during the night. If you have an MOS that has only a few training courses per year, you may have some time before your AIT training will start. In this case, you may hang around at your basic training company, leave early and wait at your AIT post or be allowed to go on leave.

For trainees in One Station Unit Training (OSUT) companies (infantry, engineers, military police), graduation activities are shortened into one or two days. Training then continues, in the same company as Advanced Individual Training (AIT). This is why your basic training is only eight weeks long.

"Basic training was tough intense training, and I'm proud of the fact that I have the physical and mental abilities to be a part of the best Army in the world."

"I believe overall I'm a better person. Now I'm more compassionate for my fellow man (or woman) due to the different conflicts and situations we've all had to endure together."

"Now that I'm graduating, I realize that basic was great because I learned something new everyday. I learned how to work with people from all over the world . . . The Army gave me the courage to be able to overcome any obstacle and anything that becomes challenging."

Chapter 6.

Five Days in the Life of a Private

This fictional diary is based on actual events, the author's observations throughout various training cycles, trainees' comments and what they and the drill sergeants have experienced:

WEDNESDAY, 6 APRIL
Dear Notebook,
I've only been in my basic training unit for a few days, and I hate it already. No one wants to work together and we're always fighting. There's this girl from the Bronx who thinks she knows everything and bosses all the other females around. She's too scared though to talk to the guys like that. OK, let me calm down. My company has about 130 privates, both male and female. My company is split up into four platoons with about 30 soldiers each. I'm in Second Platoon. You wouldn't believe how the drill sergeants were

yelling and screaming at us when we got off the cattle car. I had a military duffel bag, plus my suitcase on rollers. The drill sergeants made me carry both of them and were forcing us to run to go line up. I fell once and skinned my hand. They wouldn't even let me use the rollers on my suitcase! They made us all line up in a row and then dump all our stuff from the duffel bags on the ground! I was sweating like crazy and to make matters worse, as I dumped my duffel bag, my tampons fell out of the box and rolled everywhere. I was so embarrassed! The poor kid next to me accidentally dumped his washing detergent EVERYWHERE! We had to stand at the position of "PARADE REST", our arms crossed behind our backs, feet apart and staring straight ahead. A drill sergeant went through a list of things we were issued at the reception station, which we had to hold up one by one and then put back in the duffel bag. Imagine holding up a few pair of big, white granny underwear, and you'll know what I mean. I tried to follow along and look inconspicuous. A girl across from me started crying when a drill sergeant yelled in her face, because she couldn't find all her brown T-shirts. The drill sergeant made her do push-ups, which she couldn't do. She was too weak and couldn't even hold her body up. I could at least do five, when a drill sergeant "dropped me for push-ups", because I was supposedly "eye-balling" him.

Once we were done with that, we had to write down everything that was in our civilian bag and have a drill sergeant check it. The book I was planning to read in my free time had to be packed away. It's too bad I didn't bring a Bible. We were allowed to keep that if we had one. My platoon was on the second floor of the barracks, and it was a real challenge to drag all my bags upstairs. I was put in a room with seven other females. I quickly took the top bunk. My battle buddy, Regina, wanted the bottom bunk anyway. We had just enough time to lock our duffel bags in our wall lockers and give up our civilian bag to be locked up by the drill sergeants. We weren't going to see that again until we graduated. So much for the curling iron I brought.

We had to run back down to formation. No one knew yet where

or how we were supposed to stand, and everything was really confusing. The drill sergeants finally told us what to do. They explained some of the basic rules, especially how we're supposed to act at the dining facility. I know at this point, I was starving! We kind of marched to the mess hall and had to wait in line at "PARADE REST". I made sure that I didn't talk. I didn't want to lose my place in line. The food was pretty good, but I only had about 15 minutes to eat it. It was spaghetti with meat sauce. They even had a salad bar with all the fixings and garlic bread. I really wanted a soda, but our first glass had to be water, and I didn't even get a chance to finish that. Some guy at our table was laughing at something another private said. A drill sergeant zeroed in on him. He quickly learned what "Front, Back, Go" was. When we got back to the barracks, a drill sergeant had him outside doing "Front (push-ups), Back (flutter kicks while on your back), Go (running in place with arms out parallel to ground in front of you)". He was so out of breath he almost threw up his dinner!

After we got back in the barracks, we had just enough time to unpack and "square everything away" as the drill sergeants said, before we were given a little "free time". We had about a half an hour to get ready for bed. The drill sergeants went around and showed us how to make our bunks. My battle buddy, Regina is from Florida and she seems like she'll be OK. Tomorrow we're supposed to get up at four o'clock and do a little physical training. Later, we're going to get some classes and go to a place called CIF (Central Issue Facility) to get the rest of our gear, like our helmet and rucksack. I already want to go home, but I suppose that's normal. Well, let me try to get some sleep, I'll write when I can. Bye!

TUESDAY, 18 APRIL
Dear Notebook,
Today was the scariest day! I really dreaded it from the beginning, but you know, it wasn't so bad. We went into the gas chamber today. We had a class all morning, learning how to put our masks together, check the filters and make sure that it's ready to use.

Everyone was so quiet. Even on our latrine breaks to go to the bathroom, no one really talked with one another. I think everybody was scared.

At lunch, all the drill sergeants smiled and told us to eat a lot, even letting us get seconds on ice cream. Some drill sergeant told a private to drink a lot of milk, to coat the stomach. I though that something must be up and didn't eat too much. I had heard horror stories about that gas chamber. Well, they marched us to this little building. Some NCO in charge gave us a safety briefing and told us what we had to do. We were to put our masks on and go in the chamber ten at a time. Then we were to take our masks off and stay in there until the NCO told us to leave. By the exit, we were shown the designated area where we were supposed to go, holding our mask, flapping our hands, and WALKING, no running. Four privates were picked to stand at the entrance and the exit, to help us along. They were to go through last.

I could hear people coming out the other side, choking and coughing, which scared me even more. As I waited, I wondered if they would call an ambulance if I passed out. Then my turn came. I made sure that my mask was sealed, doing what the drill sergeants had shown us earlier. I was somewhere in the middle. Once we were in the chamber, both doors were closed. There was a fine mist floating in the air. It was really easy breathing with the mask on. Then the NCO directed us to take the mask off. I whipped mine off my head and kept my eyes closed. I tried to hold my breath, which was a mistake, the NCO was watching me. When I opened my eyes, I felt this stinging, burning sensation that brought tears to my eyes. I took a small breath and my throat just started to burn. I couldn't stop gagging, and I felt myself choking. It felt as if I was suffocating and about to throw up. My nose started to run like crazy, and I felt the saliva collecting in my mouth. My stomach was churning and it was all I could do to not throw up! That's when the door opened. We moved very quickly out that door, almost running each other over. It was all I could do to stop from rubbing my eyes.

They burned so bad! I saw guys with long strings of drool hanging from their mouths! It was so gross!

I guess it didn't affect me too bad, because, once I started looking around, I saw others collapsing on the ground, with drool and snot hanging down to the ground and just acting hysterical. A few people threw up in the chamber, which some of us had to sweep out with brooms afterwards. Later, everyone acted real cocky, and we didn't mind so much the "smoke session" (many push-ups) we got for talking.

Now, I am so sore! My muscles are aching like crazy. I just want to quit, but I know my Dad would kill me. He told me when I left, that I need to stick with it. I don't want to let him down. Today we had PT (physical training) at 4:30 AM. God, it is just so hard to get up. I still have trouble sleeping at night, tossing and turning half the night, and then I wake up dead tired. To make it worse, some idiot in our room snores!

I've been having trouble doing push-ups. I feel like I'm doing them right, but the drill sergeants say I'm mostly bobbing my head. SGT Simpson said he would work with me and not to worry. I like him the best. He actually takes the time to explain things, although if you screw up, he will still "smoke" you. That means more "Front, Back, Go".

There's this one female in my platoon who cries over everything. She gives us all a bad name. We're starting to hate her already, and I have a feeling she won't make it. Our platoon guide is this really good-looking guy, even though he has no hair. We all try to imagine what he looks like with hair. He's been really good as a platoon guide, always helpful. He knows a lot already, but that's because he did JROTC (Junior Reserve Officer's Training Corps) in high school. My battle buddy is OK, but she's so quiet. It's been hard talking to her. Well, it's the second week. Only seven more weeks to go!

FRIDAY, 11 MAY
Dear Notebook,
I shot Expert today on the rifle qualification range! I'm so happy.

I can't wait to tell my Dad! I hit 37 out of 40 targets! I finally found something that I'm pretty good at. All the guys were patting me on the back, and it really made me feel good. I was getting worried, because the third week, I was having problems with my legs, shin splints, and had to spend a few days on crutches. That's the worst. Everyone, drill sergeants and privates, treat you like a low life, who is trying to get over, if you're on some kind of code. Speaking of lowlifes, we already lost three soldiers from our platoon. The girl who kept crying was a real distracter and couldn't do anything. She was just too emotional. She was removed from training last week and spends everyday in the orderly room doing stupid paperwork stuff until she goes home. Another guy, who really wanted to be here, went on sickcall last week. He always complained that his feet hurt, and he was really getting on our nerves. Well, they diagnosed him as having bunions and he got a medical (EPTS) discharge, because he obviously had them before he got here. The other girl was always on crutches, and I don't think she ever ran with us after the initial diagnostic Basic Physical Fitness Test. She got a medical discharge for some kind of hip problem.

Now that I'm an Expert, I get to wear a special badge on my Army green uniform, the one we're wearing at graduation. The company commander pinned on the badges in a ceremony at the rifle range today. The seven other Experts and I got to wear them all day on our BDUs.

I'm keeping my fingers crossed for tomorrow. We have our third BPFT. It's called the Phase II BPFT, and we'll have one more before we graduate. My run times have really gotten good. I moved up from the slowest running group. My push-ups are getting better too. With the extra help I've been getting, I feel a lot more confident. Oh, I almost forgot. I'm also a squad leader now. I have eight people in my squad, and I'm responsible for making sure that everyone's in formation when they're supposed to be and that they have everything for the day's training.

You know, I just realized the other day that I don't want to go home anymore. This is the Sixth Week and I only have three more weeks to go. That's not that long. My battle buddy has really opened up and we're becoming fast friends. The other soldiers in my platoon aren't too bad either. I actually like getting together with them in my "free time" to practice what we've learned. Some of us have also kind of "adopted" this guy from Poland. He only came here a few years ago and still has trouble with his English, so we try to help him all we can. He's pretty smart and he fired Expert too on the range.

In a few days, we have hand grenade training and I'm really looking forward to that. We actually get to throw two live hand grenades, the same ones they throw in combat! It's off to my bunk for now. I'm sure I'll get a good night's sleep tonight, because I had fireguard last night from one 'til two in the morning, which really interrupted my sleep!

WEDNESDAY, 31 MAY
Dear Notebook,

Wow, what a long week it's been! I finally got to take a shower. I was filthy, but some of the guys stunk worse, even though they had to shave every morning. This morning, we roadmarched in from the field—15 kilometers! My feet were throbbing by the time we reached the company barracks, but I was happy! We're graduating next week! We even got ambushed on the way back. The supply sergeant and the executive officer had some M60 machine guns hiding in the bushes, and as we came around a curve, they nailed us. Everyone hit the ground, but then forgot what to do next. To make matters worse, they popped some CS gas canisters, and you should have seen some of the soldiers wildly running through the woods, trying to hold their weapon and put on their mask at the same time, which is pretty impossible. I just lay there, closed my eyes, stopped breathing and calmly put on my mask. After looking around, I noticed that cute guy who used to be the platoon guide (he got fired 'cause he screwed up the next week—we went through four platoon guides!), yelled at some of his buddies to move around the back. They were going to try to take out the M60s. I remembered this flanking movement too, so I joined them. So there we were sneaking around the back and were able to capture the M60s. We kinda saved the day, even though over half the company screwed up and either ran away or just froze.

The rest of the exercise out in the woods went a little better. Our squad became really close and I got to be squad leader a few times. I had the best time leading an ambush patrol, looking for the enemy (which was a squad from another platoon). They had on these red hats and foreign uniforms, I guess so that we wouldn't miss them. We really did a good job using the compass, hand and arm signals, and I even felt confident on the radio talking to the company commander back at the site.

I think I might have picked up some poison ivy or something. My arm is starting to get welts on in. I think I'll wait 'til tomorrow to go on sickcall. Boy, I hope I don't get any on my face! That would look horrible on graduation day. At least the drill sergeants are letting us wear make-up that day, but no bright lipstick or any nail polish.

I talked to my Dad before we went to the field, and the whole family is coming to graduation, including my grandmother from Idaho! I had to breathe a big sigh of relief after the Final Physical Fitness Test. I barely made it on the push-ups by just two push-ups. I don't know what happened. I must have been really nervous. My stomach was upset the night before, and I was really worried. Oh well, it's over for now.

I'm really going to miss all my new friends. Unfortunately, my battle buddy won't be graduating, yet. She didn't go on the roadmarch this morning, because she failed the Final Physical Fitness Test and she gets one more chance before graduation. Her problem is the run. They take the test this Saturday, and I've been praying for her and trying to help her out too. That would be awful if she wouldn't graduate. She has the same MOS as me and we're both supposed to go to Ft Lee, Virginia together!

Well, let me get to bed. They made us clean our rifles all day. They are really filthy. Not only is there all that carbon on the inside from firing all those blanks, but the outsides are just covered with crusted mud, thanks to the rain we had on the first day out. The next few days, we have to concentrate on cleaning everything, so we can turn in all our gear and our rifles. The battalion commander and some other officers are coming in to inspect it all on Monday. Talk to you again later!

TUESDAY, 6 JUN
Dear Notebook,
Well, tomorrow we graduate. I don't think I've ever been more excited in my life! I feel like a totally different person. I was so shy when I came here and now I'm just oozing confidence. I was really honored when the company commander asked me to sing the national anthem at the graduation ceremony. A few of us auditioned and me and this other guy will be singing. To tell you the truth, I'm kind of nervous. We've been practicing the last few days.

I saw my family today at a banquet the company arranged for us. I must have cried for a whole 20 minutes when I saw my Dad. I've never felt so choked up my whole life. My mom and grandmother had an ear to ear grin that whole day. It was great to be able to relax, eat some great fried chicken and talk while eating! My brother, who never gave me a compliment my whole life, actually told me I looked sharp. I'd like to say that I also lost about 10 pounds and feel great. The day was too short though, since we had to be back to the barracks at 2300 hrs (11:00 p.m.) to get ready and finish packing for graduation day.

I'm happy to say my battle buddy finally made it. I stood on the side of the track and cheered her on. She started to slow down that last lap, so I ran out on the track with her and just yelled at her. Boy, it made me feel like a drill sergeant. She barely made it on the run, but hey, she made it and we're going to AIT together.

Tomorrow, we get to sleep in about an hour. I'm looking forward to that. Then it's off to the graduation ceremony. I'm already getting butterflies about singing! Afterwards, we get to spend some more time with our families before we go to AIT. The dining facility is serving steak and shrimp, and we'll be allowed to take our families there. I think it's great we can show them where we ate, although this is the first time we're having steak and shrimp!

Oops, it's past midnight. I better get to bed! Tomorrow is going to be a long day. I can honestly say I'm going to miss this place. I've made some great friends, and I think I'll always look back fondly on my days in basic training.

Chapter 7.

Drill Sergeant Advice Column

What happens when seven drill sergeants and a command sergeant major sit around a table discussing what spells success in basic training? Sit in on their conversation and hear their advice on how you can be successful.

Command Sergeant Major Pruitt was the battalion command sergeant major of the 47th Infantry Regiment, the highest ranking NCO in the battalion. He has been in the Army over 21 years, stationed in Germany and in various posts throughout the US. He has a wealth of experience and offers his advice. These are his exact words:

"First thing, if he or she wants to come into the military, to be successful in basic combat training, I think they should consider the Army in their freshman year of high school. They have to be physically ready to take the physical fitness test. In order to do that,

I think a person has to live right, eat right, don't use a lot of alcohol, don't use any tobacco products . . . Anything bad you put in your body will decrease your chances physically, mentally and emotionally.

Mentally . . . I think that running, push-ups and sit-ups . . . are all mental. I think you can tell your body what you want it to do or what you're expected to do. When you're running around that track, if you think you're not going to make it, then you will not make it. You have to think positive, and I think your body will do what you tell it to do. You have to be able to push yourself, especially for the physical training. You have to think beyond the requirements for physical fitness in basic training, because you only have to score fifty points in each event and later you'll have to score sixty on the Army Physical Fitness Test. This means you have to increase your push-ups, sit-ups and two-mile run. So you have to ensure that you're looking towards the Army Physical Fitness Test and not just the Basic Physical Fitness Test. By the time you get to basic training, you should be close to the required number of push-ups and sit-ups it takes you to pass the diagnostic Physical Fitness Test.

Now running is a different story. I would recommend as far out in advance before I was coming to (basic training), I would start out slowly and progress up to the two-mile mark. For example, if I was just now starting out, I'd do some sort of stretching exercises . . . and run about a half-mile for a week or two and increase that . . . and even run up to five miles, but at a slower pace. Once I got to where I felt comfortable running three miles, then I would concentrate on increasing the speed, not necessarily the distance . . . It's all mental; it's in your mind.

I'm not sure that there's one memorable moment, because every day I see something that the privates do that is pretty noteworthy . . . I've seen some things that they obviously think in their mind they can't do. As far as some of the things that stick out in my mind the most, we had a private in one of the companies last cycle who came to basic training and weighed 310 pounds . . . This private, with his determination, lost 70 pounds and completed all of the requirements for basic training to include the physical fitness test. The thing that impressed me most about his determination and his willpower, was that he never gave up and continued to do those things that were required of him, particularly on the physical fitness test. When he took his first physical fitness test, I think he walked about halfway and ran about halfway. As it turned out, prior to him graduating, he was not only able to pass the physical fitness test, but he exceeded the Army standard.

Each soldier should be able to take discipline, self-discipline with them from basic training. Do the right thing in the absence of orders and do the right things without being told to do them . . . That's one of the keys to being successful in the Army. It's like I tell all the soldiers when I in-brief them. There are three things you have to do to be successful in the Army: Be where you're supposed to be, do what you're told to do and be in the right uniform. And I think, after 21 years in the Army, that's been the key to my success . . .

Oddly enough, there hasn't been much change or much difference from the privates almost twenty years ago and the expectations of them, than we have right now. The standards are a little higher now than they used to be, but generally speaking, I think we expect the same requirements from the Initial Entry Training (IET) privates now that we did twenty years ago. I think we have a much smarter Army now, a much smarter private than we had before. We have a lot coming into the Army as (the rank of Specialist) because they have college degrees. They're a lot more intelligent. They expect a lot more and it's a leadership challenge to challenge these people to give them everything that they expect.

Being a soldier is something different from being a civilian. Being a soldier is part of serving your country and doing those things that your ancestors did and that you're carrying on the traditions . . . There are a lot of success stories in basic training . . . Specifically, we've had soldiers who have come to Ft Leonard Wood who were homeless . . . from broken homes and separated families . . . and off the streets of Chicago and Philadelphia. We instill something in them . . . something they can be proud of and make a soldier out of them. It's very difficult to take a street wise person off the streets . . . who has never had any sort of discipline or any family structure or background and instill in them the discipline we require to do the right things. Those are the real success stories. It makes you feel proud to know you are part of something that *turned these people into something successful . . . The good thing about the Army, regardless of where you come from, who you are, what kind of background you have or education level you have, the Army is one place you can be successful and be whatever you want to be just like the poster says . . . You can go from Private to General in the US Army, and I think this is probably the only place in the world and in society where you can do that. The Army will train you, feed you, give you a place to live and will even pay you good money to be a soldier."*

Command Sergeant Major Dale Pruitt

Staff Sergeant McCauslin has been in the Army over 10 years and calls the Army his home. He is soft-spoken and always willing to work with any soldier. This is what he had to say:

"A lot of the soldiers come in today because of the college money and then once they get here, they're shocked. They weren't ready for the shock treatment they received, and they're lost for a few days and don't know what to do. For me, I think somebody coming in needs to realize that there's going to be a traumatic change in their life when they come here, one way or the other. They will not be the same once they leave, and they need to prepare for that.

A lot of people come here with the views from the region they live in. They need to come here realizing that not everyone was brought up the same way they were. They need to be prepared to deal with some of the different personalities and characteristics of people.

They need to have the mental toughness to say to themselves that they're not going to quit. A lot come here and within the first couple of days say they don't want to do this anymore. If this was easy, then we could just let anyone in and do away with basic training. That's the whole thing. It's not supposed to be easy; it's supposed to be hard . . . So when they come here and they're having a hard time, don't expect for someone to lower the standard or give them sympathy, because they're not making it. It's not made for everyone to get in. They're either going to have to rise up or move along.

As far as physical fitness, we need to tell these people they need to be able to perform a certain number of push-ups and sit-ups and do some running before they get here. Most of the time, what you see people hanging around and being put out (of the Army) for is physical fitness. They sit around and channel surf for most of their teenage years and then they get here and all of sudden they're expected to do . . . a whole lot at one time and that's hard, hard for them. I think it's more of a mental challenge for them than physically. They're not used to any physical exertion, and they have to get through a mental and a physical block . . . Maybe if they do a little physical activity, deal with a little discomfort to keep going, it won't be a shock when they come here and get tired, where they're not allowed to quit . . . They need to learn how to push themselves even when they think they reached that point where they're tired. That's part of mental toughness.

My most memorable experience was at graduation, during the reception. I was standing off to the side and all of a sudden, one of the soldier's fathers comes up to me and says 'I want to shake your hand . . . and I want to thank you, because prior to my son coming here, we were having a lot of troubles and since he came here he's changed a lot. I could tell he was just different, he's really grown up, and I appreciate everything you've done'. That really makes you feel good to know that you're not just making soldiers, but people—people who go out in society, not just in the front lines somewhere. I think we need to realize that besides just shooting an M16A2 (Rifle) . . . We're in a unique place with all these different cultures, where we can teach these soldiers to become better people, not just good soldiers."

Staff Sergeant Willie McCauslin

Staff Sergeant Gore is a true infantry soldier, with close to 15 years in the Army. He loves to urge privates on with his own success stories. He answers:

"Basically, before they get here, to prepare themselves for basic training, is to number one, watch their diet, watch what they eat, cut out the fat. That starts the healthy process. Then, number two is to do some kind of exercise. Start on some push-ups and sit-ups. Do something worthwhile, something consistent. Have some kind of exercise program beforehand and stay with it . . . A lot of them sit around.

THIE

They're like 'couch potatoes' and don't do any exercise. You see where their weaknesses are, whether it be in the lower extremities . . . or the chest area and a lot of them are just sitting around eating or doing nothing.

When a private comes here, some of them can't do any push-ups. One can only do five or ten sit-ups. To see that private make a turnaround, maybe a 50% or 75% raise in the standard in a matter of two to three weeks . . . that to me is the most memorable experience.

What gives me the most satisfaction is putting in 110% and watching the soldiers make the transformation from individuals off the street with no discipline, no respect, no concern about themselves or others and to watch those individuals transform through the soldierization process and to be successful at what they do, be motivated and be happy about what they're doing. That to me is very exciting."

Staff Sergeant Jerome Gore

Staff Sergeant Neese is a combat engineer by MOS, which really stands out when his company goes to the field. He can build anything out of nothing. His great sense of humor makes him a favorite with the privates. This was his first cycle. He thoughtfully replied:

"The recruiters need to develop a program to educate the new recruits on healthy lifestyles, smoking cessation, stretching exercises, getting out on running on their own and doing some push-ups and sit-ups. If they stress what it takes to pass the physical fitness test, and they can practice the physical fitness test before coming into the Army, maybe they'll be more prepared to meet the demands we put on them when they get here.

A lot of the soldiers coming in the Army today are coming in under the Delayed Entry Program (DEP), much like myself when I came in. I signed up in January, but didn't come into the Army until October. So that was ten months that I had to prepare myself, my mind and my body. I was going to do what I was going to do and come in here a little bit more prepared. Had I come in a week after I had signed up, I would not have been prepared to do that. The minimum amount of time for a soldier to prepare for basic training would be at least eight weeks.

Being a new drill sergeant, I don't have a lot of experiences to be able to pick a moment that gave me the most satisfaction. Thus far though, getting 53 individuals and watching them turn into one team, where the 53 people don't act independently, but rely on each other to get things done, start working as a team and start clicking like they're supposed to.

The shy ones, you have to get them out of their shell a little bit and those are the ones you want to put in a leadership position. That way, they have to be responsible for others' actions instead of just their own, and this boosts their confidence. They start coming out of their shell and you can see them start to put forth a little more effort.

As far as people with attitude problems. I've found the best way to handle them is to get them in the office with some other drill sergeants and use some scare tactics. Let them know that they're not the big honcho on the block anymore. Actually, sometimes they turn out to be your best soldiers. They have the leadership traits to be a leader, but just don't know how to put it in the right perspective, unless we get them under our track. Those are usually the ones you can rely on."

Staff Sergeant David Neese

Staff Sergeant Banks, one of the few female drill sergeants, is a motor transport noncommissioned officer. She is closing in on her retirement of twenty years and has enjoyed every bit of it being in the Army. She answered:

"I believe in order for a soldier to become physically and mentally prepared for basic training, doing some kind of physical activity, on a daily basis, pushing themselves to the limit is a must . . . They should start off with small goals, running three or four blocks the first day then two days later trying to increase the running distance until they are up to the two mile standard, because that's the hardest thing privates have difficulty with.

The other thing, would be to gather any kind of information concerning the military they could, like going to the library and talking with people who have retired from the military or who are in the Reserves. Get vital information from them about the living conditions, some of the things that will be expected of them. They should start trying to develop a team player's attitude, because that's one of the main things that will make them successful in basic training. They need to get in the frame of mind that sometimes they'll be discouraged, but they need to be able to motivate themselves and keep on pushing through.

When I was a private and I came in, I started approximately two months before I joined the service, and started running around the track. I started doing push-ups the best I could with my limited knowledge.

With some privates, you wonder if they've been living in cocoons their whole life and have not paid all their bills, you teach them how to dress . . . sometimes some of the things they say, you wonder, 'how did they get an idea like that'. One time, a private told a drill sergeant they wanted to sleep in late, because they didn't feel good that morning. They just come up with all kind of wild sayings."

Staff Sergeant Joanne Banks

Sergeant First Class Terry, also a motor transport noncommissioned officer, is a platoon sergeant. He rarely cracks a smile, but when he does, it's usually accompanied by a laugh that resonates throughout the barracks. He has been in the Army over twelve years and truly enjoys being a drill sergeant. He stated:

"I think when a civilian is thinking about military life they should start with exercising on their own. They should take physical education in school and really work at getting themselves physically conditioned, because it's a major problem in basic training . . . Today more kids are playing on computers and indoor games, so that means the physical conditioning of civilians is not that of what it was twenty years ago. I think the message is to get prepared, because the discipline that the Army requires you to have . . . They need to think about that they'll have an authority figure in charge of them once they get here, and maybe they weren't used to that back in civilian life. They were able to talk back to their teachers or their parents, and in the military, you won't be allowed to do that. So, you need to get in the right mindset, prior to getting here and be willing to except it.

I think the most memorable experience you can have as a drill sergeant in basic training, is graduation day of each cycle, because you see that civilian who showed up Day One of basic training transformed into a soldier eight weeks later and to see the expression on the parents' faces when they arrive and see that you made a difference. It's a whole different outlook to see the parents see the difference that you made . . . and you can really have an impact on a group of people, even if you only reach one. How many other jobs can you have where you can transform a person into something different?"

Sergeant First Class Gregory Terry

Sergeant First Class Tircuit, perhaps one of the most interesting drill sergeants, started out in the Army playing a horn. That's right. He was a musician. Later in his career, he changed over to the Nuclear, Chemical and Biological (NBC) MOS. He's dealt with all kinds of deadly chemicals and was confident in tackling any kind of obstacle in basic training. He said:

"The recruiter knows what is expected to pass basic training. For example I had a friend, divorced with three kids. In order to prepare for basic training she went to the gym, three or four times a week. She ran on her own. She did push-ups and sit-ups. She got the sergeants (recruiters) to help her out. When she went to Ft Jackson (basic training), she won the physical fitness award, because she had practiced earlier and the sergeants were able to tell her what to do to pass.

Mentally, the biggest thing is about being disciplined and not giving up. People come here and they give up on the first physical fitness test, or the first run. They can't take orders. A lot of people are not mature. If you really want something, you can do it. You just have to work hard at it . . . Basic training is not designed to be easy. It is designed to test your ability, your will to go on, no matter what—the roadmarches, physical training, the basic rifle marksmanship, whatever classes you have . . .

This cycle, what really stuck out in my mind was a private who had trouble shooting. She had to go to the range a few times to qualify and the last time she came back, she didn't qualify and she cried, but she came to me and asked what she could do. She was determined. So the day she qualified I was very proud, because I knew how hard she had worked."

Sergeant First Class Sergeant Alonzo Tircuit

Staff Sergeant Lynch is an infantryman. There is no doubt about this as he goes about his work. He lets the trainees know who is boss and never gives an inch. He states:

"To start out, mentally, a person must prepare himself to be able to take orders and to be able to execute those orders to the best of his ability, regardless of the situation of how he feels or how difficult the task may be. The physical preparation, (the soldier) basically needs to start from the very first moment you even dream of coming into the military. If it means getting involved in athletics in your school programs or getting out and doing different kinds of exercises on your own. Touch bases with physical fitness trainers, coaches, those kinds of personnel can help you tremendously in preparing yourself.

I can honestly say my most memorable experience . . . would be my very first graduation, not the graduation itself but the tremendous sense of accomplishment I felt seeing those privates marching in a graduation ceremony. It just made you feel so good to see the finished product—a person changed from a civilian into a soldier. That is the most tremendous feeling I think I have ever felt or ever will feel while here at basic training."

Staff Sergeant Charles Lynch

CHAPTER 8.

GETTING DISCHARGED FROM THE MILITARY

Every cycle, anywhere from 2-10% of the soldiers in a class are discharged. As you know, a class in a cycle averages anywhere from 110 to 250 soldiers. There are two main types of discharges, or chapters, commonly used in basic training to discharge a trainee. The first, Existing Prior to Service (EPTS), Chapter 5-11 is initiated by the military medical community, the second, an Entry Level Separation (ELS), Chapter 11, the company commander initiates. Any soldier who has been in the Army under six months can be discharged under either of these chapters. For soldiers who have been in the military longer than six months, and out of basic training, different chapters are used for their discharge that won't be discussed here.

THE EXISTING PRIOR TO SERVICE (EPTS) MEDICAL DISCHARGE

EPTS, Chapter 5-11 discharges are characterized by medical problems the soldier had that existed prior to him entering the service. The majority of discharges from basic training fall under Existing Prior to Service (EPTS), Chapter 5-11 discharges. Listed below are some of the most frequent reasons trainees are discharged under EPTS:

- Asthma (diagnosed through a series of respiratory tests)
- Shortness of breath (diagnosed through a series of respiratory tests)
- Orthopedic problems (usually lower back, shoulder, knees, ankles, etc)

Other reasons trainees have been discharged in the past included: bunions, endometriosis, manic depression, chronic rashes, pregnancy, bipolar disorder and scleroderma. Most likely, if you are put on medication to control your condition (such as a mental condition or asthma) or are pregnant, you will be discharged. This is also not a comprehensive list of all the reasons that will get you discharged. If you are still unsure, use this as a "rule of thumb". If you go to the medical facility and complain about your condition, whatever it is, chances are high you will be recommended for discharge by the medical facility if you are unable to cope with your condition or if it interferes with your training.

The first run a company conducts is a good indicator of those trainees having some kind of a physical problem. A few always complain about breathing problems and are unable to keep up, even though the group runs at a fairly slow pace, about 15-18 minutes per mile in a mixed gender company. Some trainees actually fall to the ground and have to be assisted to get up. Of course, sometimes this may be more for the dramatic effect. Report in good physical condition, and this won't be you. Others notice after a few days that their feet, legs, hips or other body parts hurt more than seems normal. These are usually people who have led a mostly sedentary lifestyle, or have sometime in their past, had a significant injury that never healed properly. Some overtrain in the few weeks before basic training, and their bones are beginning to show the stress now. Of course, many of these trainees go on sickcall and are diagnosed with some kind of medical condition that will take time to heal. As soon as a doctor diagnoses the condition, and it is determined the condition existed before the trainee entered the Army, the trainee goes through a medical board to determine if this limitation will allow him to remain in the Army. More often than not, the trainee is deemed unfit for military service and is discharged within three to six weeks with no benefits. They may always try to re-enter the military if they are able to "fix" their medical condition at their own expense.

Now, do not get a prior injury confused with an injury you received while in basic training. Trainees who are injured or become sick while in the Army, are given the time to recover from their injuries or illness and then are "new started" into a basic training company that is in the same week of training that you previously completed. Of course, you could always get "new started" at the beginning of a basic training cycle if too much time has gone by. If the injuries do not heal in a reasonable timeframe or the illness leaves them unable to finish training (anywhere from two to six months), the soldier may be scheduled to attend a board hearing, where it will be determined if he can stay in the Army. If these trainees are recommended for discharge, they often receive some kind of disability compensation and are eligible for other Veteran's benefits.

THE ENTRY LEVEL SEPARATION (ELS) DISCHARGE

The other discharge frequently used by a basic training company commander is the Entry Level Separation (ELS), Chapter 11. This is used as a last resort. If a trainee is continuously disruptive or unable to integrate into the Army environment, this type of discharge is used. Listed below are some of the actual cases where trainees have been discharged under Chapter 11:

- Trainee threatened other privates and was continuously disruptive in class, actually pointing a rifle at a fellow private
- Trainee cried all the time and while marching to training, would try to slip away from the company
- Trainee knowingly and repeatedly did not follow orders
- Trainee stole some items from the Post Exchange (PX) the day after graduation

TRAINEES HAVING PROBLEMS ADJUSTING

The Army has many agencies available to counsel trainees to get over their initial shock of being in the Army. Almost every trainee, in the first few weeks of training, feels like quitting and giving up. The first step in dealing with these trainees is counseling the individuals who really seem to have a problem adjusting. It is always reiterated to them, that they signed a legal, binding contract that they must uphold. It is their obligation to abide by the terms of their contract. As mentioned earlier, they also get an opportunity to speak with the chaplain and counselors from the mental health/

psychiatric facility. Throughout this process, they are encouraged by their drill sergeants and other company cadre to continue to train. Most of the time, this counseling helps a soldier get over this initial adjustment disorder, as the Army calls it, and they are able to train.

A Soldier Who Stuck With It

The company commander was sitting in the dining facility, watching her new soldiers go through the chow line. One of the drill sergeants came to her and pointed out a private, who was acting very strange. She was pushing privates out of the way to get to the front of the line. As she was getting her food, she was stuffing it in her mouth with her hands. Her face looked like a chipmunk. Even though her mouth was full, she kept stuffing more and more food into it. When she went to sit down, she would not listen to drill sergeants telling her to slow down. The cadre were concerned that she might start choking. Later that day, she acted very disoriented, telling a drill sergeant she was in a different room and that he was not her drill sergeant. She spoke incoherently and was later found hiding in a wall locker. After the commander spoke with her, she found out that this was the private's first time away from home. PVT Walsh was counseled by everyone in the chain of command, and was able to overcome her problems. She became the model soldier and graduated with honors, even qualifying "Sharpshooter" on her M16A2.

Of course, counseling doesn't help everyone. When all attempts at counseling and disciplinary action have failed, the commander will recommend the trainee be discharged under an Entry Level Separation (ELS). Under the discharge, the trainee does not receive any benefits. It takes from three to six weeks to send a private home. With this type of discharge, a person can always try to re-enter the military after two years. Many privates discharged under ELS are either emotionally immature or rebellious in nature and are unable to adapt to a military environment.

HIE

OTHER TYPES OF DISCHARGES

A commander, any Army commander, has a variety of other discharges that are available to him. A basic training company commander is not just limited to the two mentioned above. One particular trainee at Ft Leonard Wood was discharged under Chapter 6, Hardship Discharge, because her husband abandoned the children at home and there was no one available to care for them while she attended basic training. This type of discharge requires extensive documentation. The help of the Red Cross and local social workers at the soldier's home were enlisted to verify authenticity.

Lastly, a small percentage of trainees have been discharged under Chapter 15, Homosexuality. The Army's policy is very specific on reasons a soldier can be discharged under Chapter 15. A trainee either has to make a statement that he is homosexual, perform a homosexual act or marry a person of the same sex. The Army does not seek out homosexuals. Only when a trainee approaches a drill sergeant with a difficulty of being able to cope in the Army as a homosexual, must it be investigated. The legal process is long in discharging a soldier for homosexuality and can involve many sensitive questions and issues. In many of the homosexuality cases, trainees mention they were extremely uncomfortable showering and changing around so many men. They also felt a sense of closeness to other male trainees that interfered with their concentration to train. In my experience as a commander, I only discharged 2-4 homosexuals who were male in a 12-month timeframe. All of these trainees approached their drill sergeants and their chain-of-command directly. Females can also be discharged under this chapter if they come forward.

CHAPTER 9.

COED TRAINING

If you will be attending basic training at Ft Knox or Ft Benning, you will not be "gender integrated" and will be in an "all male" unit. OSUT (One Station Unit Training) in the Combat Arms is also not "gender integrated" as this field is not open to women. Combat Engineers is the only Combat Arms exception where women are now being admitted. The Army first tried "gender integrated" training (training men and women together) from 1978 to 1982, but ended it because it was believed the male recruits weren't challenged enough. "Gender integrated" training was begun again in 1993 at Ft Jackson, South Carolina, and is most likely here to stay. There is still disagreement to this day over this change. As with everything, there are two sides to every story. Below are the major reasons you will hear for the proponents of coed training and those against it.

SPEAKING AGAINST COED TRAINING

Opponents like to say that females being trained together with males, slows down the development of the male as a soldier. The males will not be able to bond. Females are distracters and slow down the males during physical training as well. Too many changes have to be made in the living and latrine facilities, and extra care has to be taken with both sexes living so close together. The trainees will occupy their minds with sex and finding a mate or sex partner. There will be too many rapes. Women will entice the males.

SPEAKING FOR COED TRAINING

Advocates of training males and females together say that the Army has to wake up and get into the 20th century. How can males and females be expected to work together efficiently when they arrive in their first unit, if they didn't start their Army careers working together? These trainees worked together in high school and throughout their life, why not now? Training together brings out the best in both sexes, especially the competition factor. Before integrated training, it was very difficult to train an "all female" company. Many drill sergeants dreaded it. Some females showed little motivation to excel and tried to manipulate the mostly male drill sergeants. This is a pretty harsh statement, but there are drill sergeants out there who believe this. A few female soldiers thought that if they cried and batted their eyelashes a little, drill sergeants would give them a break and not be so hard on them. If male trainees start training early in their careers with females, they would not develop the antiquated idea that females are inferior. Being around a majority of males, females will not be prone to try and manipulate drill sergeants. Males and females are supposed to be getting the same training. How can they get the same training if they're separated? Is this the separate but equal concept again?

THE AUTHOR'S OBSERVATIONS OF COED TRAINING

It was noticed that most of the time, males and females complement each other. For instance, males seem to push themselves more in the presence of females. Most males work especially hard to make themselves look like they know what they're doing in front of females. It's possible they do not want to be embarrassed. If a female has no trouble throwing a live grenade, how could a male then show his fear of the grenade? Females consistently do better in subjects where attention to detail is required. Females typically take up the role as teacher, tutoring the males. Many females tend to be more patient and more willing to help those who aren't doing as well. As a whole, females do better on written tests. The males tend to excel in physically challenging events, where strength is required, as well as the long roadmarches.

There are only two real downsides observed with "gender integrated" training. The first is the higher injury rate of females. The Army is currently conducting studies into this problem, which only recently came about in such great numbers with "gender integrated" training. Possibly, the female lesser bone density combined with the increased levels of physical fitness training, could be the cause of this high injury rate. It is not unusual to have four to six females on crutches the second week of training, due to signs of stress fractures. Being around a lot of males, most females tend to ignore the warning signs from their body to slow down and push themselves too hard.

The second downside, with males and females living so close together, is the temptation to start some kind of interaction of a sexual nature. Not everyone can be mature about this subject and act responsibly. Frequently, a male or female soldier causes disruptions by being either promiscuous or assaulting or confronting members of the opposite sex. This takes the focus away from training.

SEXUAL HARASSMENT

Sexual harassment is and always will be a volatile issue in the military. More and more emphasis has been put on this issue in the Army. It is a general belief that sexual harassment training must begin early in the Army—in basic training. Many trainees were never taught anything about sexual harassment in school or at home. Sexual harassment is when someone continues to make sexual comments/advances towards someone else after they have asked you to stop. The problem with sexual harassment is that everyone has their own tolerance of what is accepted. For example, some people may not be bothered by sexual jokes. On the other hand, some are so sensitive, that any touch from the opposite sex will cause them to feel harassed. The best advice is to not make sexual comments or to touch anyone in a sexual way. If someone tells you to stop, then immediately stop from doing it again.

COED LIVING CONDITIONS

You're probably wondering how males and females live under the same roof together and how they are integrated. For starters, all trainees live in the same barracks buildings. Some companies have all females stay on one floor, others integrate them on each floor. On integrated floors, there might be a female room next to a male room. Depending on the size of the room, anywhere from two to sixteen trainees may live there. After "lights out", males cannot go into female rooms and vice versa. Trainees sleep in their physical fitness uniforms. They must change clothes in the latrines. This proves to be an inconvenience, but without rebuilding barracks space, this is how "gender integrated" living currently works.

COED DAILY TRAINING

Both sexes participate in training together. The only instance where they might be separated, is to receive instruction in personal hygiene and breast/prostate cancer screening. Drill sergeants sometimes do this to encourage discussion, since some people are a little shy in discussing certain issues in front of the other sex. The sexes are again separated when they receive their Army green uniform, which they wear at graduation. Both sexes are given the opportunity to be in platoon and squad leadership positions and are expected to carry the same workload. For example, there is no difference in the amount of weight in a female or a male's rucksack. Both sexes fire the same rifle, wear the same BDUs and physical fitness uniforms. Currently, the unofficial standard for the male/female ratio in each company is 75:25 at "gender integrated" training posts. Of course, this can't always be achieved due to recruiting missions, but it's something the Army strives for. This mix tends to bring out the best in both sexes.

Two female trainees being "as bad as they wanna be" during the hand-to-hand combat training. The drill sergeants will pick your same sex opponent, and you'll have a go at it!

COMMENTS FROM TRAINEES ON COED TRAINING

Here are some comments from some former trainees on "gender integrated" training. Interestingly enough, most of the negative comments were made by males. Most females were happy with the new system, feeling the joint training pushed them to do even better.

"The only major thing I would change about my training is the mixture of males and females. It only caused fights amongst the soldiers and took some of their minds off training. It made it hard to live with females, because even though I've trained not to treat them different, it was hard to do that. It was hard to encourage somebody who was always in tears, because the pressure or stress was too hard on them."

"I don't know how long integrated training has been in effect, or how well it has been working. I myself have mixed feelings about it.

I have noticed advantages and disadvantages. During my training here I have noticed that the female soldiers do add a lot to platoons discussions and propose interesting questions. But on the other hand physically, a lot of the females fall short. Not that there are no weak males. My point actually is that along with the integrated training I would like to see the soldiers also split into ability groups before basic training."

"On integrated training, it was felt that there was something added and lost. The fact that women and men trained side by side was a bonus, in that male soldiers learned that they could depend on the other sex in times of turmoil and trouble. It was interesting to see some rather physically fit women and weak men in the battle of the sexes, and the continued growing confidence that women could do the same jobs as men. The flip side . . . found male soldiers rather annoyed with drill sergeants, because it was felt that the female soldiers were being given favoritism and other special treatment. I will assure you though that this soldier saw no sign of the above, and I felt that everyone was treated equally."

"To me, the most shocking difference and the one thing which I reject, is training and living with females. I feel that at least 40% of both sexes' concentration is lost from training due to trying to impress or look good in front of one or the other. The males' training is reduced as there are things that females just can't keep up with, the feeling of 'bonding' in the unit is lost and too much time and effort is spent concentrating on ethics and proper conduct."

"Many of my fellow battle buddies complained about the integrated training. I also complained, because I was under the impression that we should train males with males and females with females. I saw too many fellow soldiers forgetting what they came here for . . . I didn't come here to find a girlfriend, I came here to train for combat."

"I believe that basic training would have been more beneficial to both sexes if male and female soldiers were separated. It would cut down a lot on distractions, which a lot of time holds trainees back from reaching their potential, not to mention the Article 15s which can stack up on the commander's desk."

"For me, the barracks arrangement . . . was all washed up. It was

like putting a weasel in the henhouse for some that were not well disciplined. That can be distracting because you find yourself caught between, do I tell on my battle buddy for misconduct or do I let it continue, without messing with their careers . . . The right thing to do is to tell, but I personally don't like snitches. To correct this problem, I feel the males and females should be on separate floors, maybe with the Charge of Quarters between them. The first thing I think of with that suggestion is why do we have to treat grown people like teenagers? Probably, because most of them are not mature enough or disciplined enough to do as they are told."

"I didn't like coed platoons . . . for many reasons. As a male, I thought they would get by with a lot more stuff . . . I don't think I ever hardly saw a female get dropped. It was really hard not to talk to them like you were at home . . . This was a constant friction between the males and the females. I think we should have separate platoons."

"When I enlisted, I did not know basic training was coed . . . I would have liked to have had a male only basic because it seems there were extra restrictions because of the females and interacting with them was dangerous because of sexual harassment issues."

You can make up your own mind about training males and females together, but in today's society, it is probably here to stay. There are basic training posts that still train male-only companies, specifically, Combat Arms basic training, such as infantry and armor. As long as women are not allowed into some Combat Arms specialties, they obviously will not attend these branches' basic training. Throughout the Army, there are also no more all-female companies. They have all been combined into "gender-integrated" companies.

CHAPTER 10.

FREQUENTLY ASKED QUESTIONS

Do you still have questions that weren't answered? Here are some questions trainees have actually asked and some they may have wanted to ask but were afraid to.

Q: What exactly are the requirements to enter the Army?

A: Here are the minimum enlistment standards:

- Must be at least 17 years old and not have reached 35th birthday by the date of accession. A 17-year-old who has not reached his or her 18th birthday at the time of enlistment must have parental consent in writing.
- Must pass a physical and moral screening.
- Must have qualifying Armed Forces Qualification Test (AFQT) score and Army Composite Scores on the Armed Services Vocational Aptitude Battery (ASVAB).
- Must be a US citizen or registered alien.
- Army prefers to enlist high school diploma graduates. GEDs are accepted.

Q: Why are there other trainees running around basic training with a higher rank than me? I saw one guy who was a Private First Class, what's up?

A: Not everyone enters the Army as a private (E-1). If you have any education beyond high school, you may be eligible to enter at a higher rank. These are known as accelerated promotions:

As Private 2 (E-2)—30-59 semester hours

As Private First Class (E-3)—60+ semester hours

As Specialist (E-4)—Bachelor's degree

If you are a Boy Scout who has achieved the rank of Eagle Scout or a Girl Scout who has earned the Gold Award Certificate and are a high school graduate, you may enlist as a Private 2 (E-2). An active duty soldier can also refer you into the Army, in the rank of Private 2 (E-2) under the Delayed Entry Program (DEP). Ask your recruiter if you think you may be eligible.

Q: I came to basic training in the summer and was surrounded by all these kids who were juniors in high school. How did they get in the Army?

A: These high school kids are known as "split-option soldiers" and are Reservists. They sign a contract with the Army to go to basic training after their junior year of high school. After they go back to school to finish their senior year, they move on to attend their AIT.

Q: Is Army pay really comparable to what I'd be getting paid in the civilian world?

A: Yes, yes and more so! Not only do you get what's called a base pay for your "time in service" and your rank, you get other benefits too. You get tax-free allowances, clothing, housing, food, medical and dental coverage, legal assistance and tax-free shopping. Now is there any civilan job out there that can offer you all that extra?

Q: I just want to know when I will get paid and how?

A: Your paycheck will be electronically sent to the bank account of your choice, twice a month. You will receive a Leaves and Earnings Statement (LES), when you are paid. This statement shows how much you were paid, the taxes taken out of your check, any deductions, allotments you have going to other accounts and how much vacation time (or leave) you have earned. You receive a base pay, which everyone at your rank and time in the service gets. You will get extra money if you have dependents (spouse and/or children). Once you are out of basic training and AIT you may get other additions, depending on whether you eat your meals in a dining facility, live on post, or off post. Deductions may include a dental plan for your dependents and/or Serviceman's Group Life Insurance (SGLI). Allotments are special payments you have designated to go to another source, such as savings accounts, mutual funds or child support payments. Your earned vacation days, also known as "leave", are annotated on the statement also.

Q: How much will I be getting paid?

A: This chart, effective July 1, 2000, is the base pay each month. It does not include any additional payments, such as money for housing (BAH) or subsistence allowance for food (BAS).

Rank	Pay
Private (less than 4 months)	$930.30
Private (over 4 months)	$1005.60
Private 2 (E-2)	$1127.40
Private First Class (E-3)	$1171.50
Specialist (E-4)	$1249.90

If you have dependents (a spouse and/or children), you are entitled to Basic Allowance for Housing (BAH). This amount is based on their geographic location, your pay grade and the status of your dependents.

Q: Okay, you mentioned that I earn vacation days in the Army. How many days can I take off a year? Can I take a vacation whenever I want?

A: You earn or accrue 2.5 days a month, which adds up to 30 paid vacation days a year! That's better than any civilian job can offer you! Now, you won't be able to take off whenever you want to though. Permission must be granted by your supervisor and commanding officer, and this always depends on mission requirements. Let's say your unit is going on a big training exercise during the week you want to go on vacation (or leave, as the Army calls it). Chances are, you won't be able to go then, because you're needed at your job. Of course, in basic training, you won't be allowed to go on vacation at all. Drill sergeants like to say, this is your vacation. Most trainees go on their first vacation after they complete AIT. If your AIT is long, such as over 10 weeks, you can usually take about a week long vacation before you get there.

Q: Why don't the company commander and first sergeant wear drill sergeant hats (similar to Smokey the Bear hats)?

A: The drill sergeant hat must be earned and can only be worn while on drill sergeant status. The Drill Sergeant School is about two months long and can only be attended by non-commissioned officers. This makes officers such as the company commander, a captain, ineligible.

Q: What is in this Initial Entry Training (IET) Handbook that is so important and when can I get a copy?

A: You will receive this small handbook at the reception station. You will always be required to carry it around in your pocket and during every small break or during "down time" you will be required to get it out and to read it! The book contains the basic information that you will need to know as an Army private and also includes some tasks that you must be proficient in before graduating. Some of the subjects include: the Army song,

Army organization, rank insignia, military time, salutes and honors, basic soldier skills, Army core values and lots of Army tidbits of knowledge. If you want to get a head start and look at the book beforehand, you can find it at http://www.adtdl.army.mil/cgi-bin/atdl.dll/pam/600-4/tp600-4.htm. This will be the only "textbook" you will receive in basic training, along with a few photocopied handouts and worksheets.

Q: I'm a vegetarian and am worried about the food choices available?
A: Every meal has a salad and/or fruit bar. Potatoes are served every day, as well as a variety of other vegetables. Other vegetarians have been able to find something at every meal, although during a field chow, choices can be slim.

Q: I'm a Muslim and don't eat pork products. Will this be a problem?
A: There must be at least two meat choices at every meal, one of which must not be pork.

Q: I've been practicing sit-ups and sometimes I can't keep myself from passing gas and grunting! I'm dreading being embarrassed?
A: Don't worry, you'll find others who inadvertently pass gas or grunt. This is normal. Just excuse yourself and you'll be okay. Remember, you won't be the only one, and you can laugh about it later.

Q: Will I be able to pick a roommate?
A: No. A battle buddy will be assigned to you, and hopefully, this private will be assigned to your room. Depending on the barracks structure, you may have anywhere from one to 15 roommates.

Q: I've never fired a weapon before, and I'm afraid I won't do well! What should I do to prepare?
A: The best way to prepare yourself now, is to ensure your eyesight is in order. If you have trouble seeing now, get glasses and get used to wearing them. You won't be allowed to wear contact

lenses. In case your military glasses don't fit quite right, you'll have your civilian glasses as a backup. Don't worry about firing your weapon and qualifying. The Army teaches you everything from the ground up. If you pay attention in class and on the firing ranges, you will do well. Some drill sergeants say they can teach a monkey to shoot.

Q: Can I wear my contacts?

A: No. While in training you absolutely cannot wear these due to health and safety reasons. Once you graduate from Advanced Individual Training (AIT), and you are assigned to your Army unit, you may wear them.

Q: I've never done anything physical my whole life! I'm scared about running. What if I can't keep up?

A: You must start getting in shape now. There's nothing worse than running for the first time in basic training if you've never run before. Your body will resist. Some trainees fall on the ground, out of breath, complain about everything hurting and a few even lose their lunch!. It also feels pretty low to see the rest of the company leaving you in the dust. Many privates need extra time to heal strained muscles, which is pretty impossible in nine short weeks. You'll get left behind! It's also pretty miserable to see your friends graduate and you didn't because you did not pass your final physical fitness test. Don't allow yourself to be put in this situation. Get in shape now!

Q: Will we have any free time?

A: In the first three weeks, your free time will be structured. In the evenings, you will have about an hour from the end of chow or reinforcement time until lights out. Drill sergeants will break this hour into increments, such as fifteen minutes for shining boots, fifteen minutes writing letters home, etc. Starting the fourth week, you have more control over what you do, but cannot leave the barracks area. Later in the cycle, you may be given the opportunity to go to the mini-PX under drill sergeant supervision. The only real free time you have is during church services and right before graduation.

Q: The chaplain sure briefed us on a lot of different church services. I never even heard of over half the religions mentioned. I'm not very religious. What am I going to do when everyone goes to church?

A: There will be others who don't want to go to any services. You'll stay in the barracks area and be kept busy by drill sergeants or given some time to yourself. Most privates try to sneak a nap, clean up their area or write letters home.

Q: Will I be able to read what I want in my free time? What if my family sends me a package with cookies and candy?

A: Only religious material is allowed, although some companies allow you to read your hometown newspaper if it's delivered to you. Don't bother forwarding your catalogs or magazine subscriptions. Drill sergeants will put these away. For most of the training cycle, drill sergeants confiscate any candy or cookies. If your mom insists on sending cookies, tell her to wait until you're closer to graduation.

Q: I'm shy. I'm a little worried about taking showers and using the bathroom with others in the latrine? How do I get around this?

A: Well, there's no room to be shy about your body here. The showers are all in one big stall, and since there are not enough shower heads for each trainee, be prepared to share one with someone. It's general practice to soap yourself up, while someone else is under the water and then you switch. It shouldn't take more than three minutes. Some privates try to shower before lights out in the evening, when they have more time. This works occasionally, but you'll still be hot and sweaty after physical training in the morning. As far as the bathroom goes, back in the old days, there weren't any stalls or walls around the toilets.

A former retired colonel the author knows, waited until everyone was asleep and then went to the bathroom. Well, he wasn't the only one who had that idea. The place was a high traffic area as soldiers walked in and out in the wee hours of the morning, doing their duty so to speak. Today, there are at least doors to offer a little more privacy.

Q: Can I bring photos with me?
A: Of course. Many soldiers put up pictures of family, boyfriends and girlfriends on the inside of their wall locker. Just make sure they're in good taste.

Q: What if the Army can't keep its side of the bargain and my MOS or the options I picked are no longer available? Can this happen to me during basic training?
A: There have been some soldiers in the past, who were unable to attend the AIT they had previously selected. Occasionally, the Army is unable to uphold its commitment to you. In this case, you can either choose another available MOS for which you are qualified or another station or unit, or be released from your Army contract with no strings attached.

Q: I'm only 4'11' tall. I'm worried about keeping up with some of those big guys.
A: Unfortunately, you will have to work that much harder to keep up with the taller trainees. During runs and roadmarches, it may take you two steps for every one of their steps. Your rucksack and weapon may be a little overwhelming at first. But, typically the shorter trainees show more determination and motivation to succeed. It's how you perceive yourself in your mind. If you think you can't keep up, then you won't be able to.

Q: Can I bring/wear sunglasses?
A: No, no, no. Unless the Army issues you a pair (which you won't see in basic training), the pair you brought with you will be packed away.

Q: Can I bring a camera and take pictures?
A: You will have to pack it away if you bring it. You may be allowed to use it during the graduation activities. Like every private who came before you, you will be bombarded to buy a yearbook, video, platoon and individual photos while you're here. To some, you're just a walking dollar sign. You'll have plenty of memories to take with you, if you're willing to spend a little money. If it's a cheap camera, bring it. You may be able to use it closer to graduation week.

Q: I'm not ready to cut my hair short? Can I wear hair ribbons or barrettes?
A: If you have to put your hair up, the rubberbands and barrettes must be the same color as your hair. No ponytails are allowed, and you cannot use brightly colored hair accessories. You either have to braid your hair or put it in a tucked-under ponytail.

Q: Do all males have to get their heads shaved? I kind of have a funny shaped head?
A: Get prepared. Get used to a short haircut now. If you have pretty long hair now, it will be an even bigger shock when your head gets shaved. Your head will be shaved throughout basic training. You might get lucky and have a longer cut for graduation, which means a little up top.

Q: What's it like sleeping in the woods?
A: In the summer it will be miserably hot and if you don't use bug juice (insect repellent), the bugs will eat you alive. In addition to mosquitos, you might get ticks and chigger bites, or maybe even poison oak or ivy. In the winter, you will most likely be distracted from training due to the cold. You will be sharing a pup tent with your battle buddy and have barely enough room to turn around in your sleep. Forget sitting up; there is no headroom. It's definitely an experience you won't forget. You will join one of the oldest clubs in the Army, those who hate going to the field and those who relish it.

Q: How will I wash my clothes?

A: Although there are washing machines and dryers in the barracks, you won't be able to wash all your clothes in them. You will not have the time, and you need to share these limited appliances with the other privates. Sign up for quartermaster laundry, which is a service the Army provides at a cost. The cost of this service is conveniently taken out of your paycheck every month. Send all your heavy duty items, such as your uniforms and brown t-shirts to quartermaster laundry. Try to launder things like underwear, socks and physical fitness uniforms in the barracks. Quartermaster laundry is a big place and there are frequently privates who get back only one sock, or worse yet, someone else's underwear. The Quartermaster laundry system is contracted out by the Army and is unfortunately far from perfect.

Q: Because of my MOS, I think I'll be going to a coed basic training post. Where are they located?

A: Currently, the three "gender-integrated" basic training posts are Ft Jackson, SC; Ft Leonard Wood, MO and recently also Ft Sill, OK. One Station Unit Training (OSUT) is training where basic training and advanced individual training (AIT) are conducted together in the same company. OSUT companies are located in Ft Benning, GA (Infantry); Ft Knox, KY (Armor); Ft Leonard Wood, MO (Combat Engineers, Military Police and Chemical) and Ft Sill, OK (Field Artillery). The non-combat arms OSUT companies, such as Chemical and Military Police, do have "gender-integrated" companies. Combat Engineers and Field Artillery, both Combat Arms branches, have recently started admitting women also and training them in integrated companies.

Q: My mother is fairly ill, and I'm worried about leaving her. What's the best way for my family to reach me if my mother's illness has complications?

A: Normally, trainees are allowed to use the phone once or twice a week for a few minutes at a time. Since you will be out training everyday, you won't be able to receive any phone calls and there is no answering service. Now for emergencies, there is a different procedure. The fastest way your family can reach you is to call their local Red Cross chapter, who in turn calls the Red Cross on your training post. Make sure your family knows where you'll be assigned and the name of your unit. Within the day, you can be on a plane home if necessary. Some training units also have email and websites. Use the email only for emergencies.

Q: Will I be able to call home when I get to my company?
A: Within 72 hours of arriving, you will be given this opportunity. Calls will most likely be limited to only a few minutes. The whole company will probably be waiting in line behind you.

Q: My fiancee insists she wants to try to come visit me. What should I tell her?
A: It's not a good idea to have anyone visiting you here. You won't have the time! Tell her you will spend time with her the day before graduation. Company commanders are very strict about this policy. Can you imagine how angry your fiancee would be if she drove all the way to see you and was turned away?

Q: How do I let my family know about graduation and any other privileges I might be getting?
A: During your company in-processing, you will send form letters home, detailing some basic information they might be interested in, as well as the schedule of events for the graduation activities. Some companies have websites, even uploaded training schedules and current photos from the training being conducted.

Q: How will my parents know where to write me? What's my address?
A: Again, the form letter sent home will have your full address in it. Most units no longer require that the soldier's SSN be printed on the envelope for security reasons. Training companies also request that you try to refrain from sending registered or certified

mail, as this can take the soldier away from training to go sign for it. The exact mailing address depends on what unit you will be assigned to, but the basic format is:

PVT Schmo, Joe
Company, Battalion (Platoon)
Street Address
City, State ZIP

Q: Do we get special vacation time around Christmas and New Years? I'll be going to basic training in November.

A: Most basic training posts stop training around mid-December and give you a chance to take leave until the first week of January. This break is called Christmas Exodus. If you don't have a place to go or want to save money, the barracks will stay open and you'll be allowed to attend different holiday activities. You'll be given advance pay to pay for travel expenses, which will be deducted from your paycheck at the end of the month. Since you probably won't have a lot of leave time accrued at this point, you will end up owing the Army leave time. You will then have to gain it back, 2.5 days for every month you're in the Army.

Q: When can I expect to get my first promotion?

A: It takes about six months on active duty to advance to Private Two (E-2) and about twelve months to make Private First Class (E-3). Your commander also has the authority to promote three percent of your graduating class to E-2.

Q: I'm having second thoughts about going to college. Can I take some college classes while I'm in the Army?

A: After you graduate AIT and report to your first duty station, you will have a variety of degrees and educational programs open to you. This is the Army's Continuing Education Program. Many soldiers take college courses in their off-duty time to earn degrees and further their education.

Q: Wow, all these acronyms! I'm getting to know some of them and wondered what TA-50 is?

A: TA-50 is just the gear that is issued to you from the Central Issue Facility (CIF). Yep, more acronyms! In basic training, this gear looks pretty beat up, as you can imagine all the trainees who used it before you! You'll get things like canteens, pistol belt, raingear, rubber boots, ammunition pouches, Kevlar helmet and a shelter half (your half of the tent you share with your buddy), to name a few things. Basically, this gear will fill two large duffel bags and be very heavy!

Q: My neighbor just wrote me about basic training and kept talking about these Army Core Values. My Dad, a proud basic training graduate, never heard of those. What's up with that?

A: In the last two years, the Army has started teaching these values to basic training soldiers in the hopes of instilling in them a sense of these values to live by the rest of their Army career. They are: loyalty, duty, respect, selfless service, honor, integrity and personal courage. These values will be "hammered into your brain" by the time you graduate. If you want to get a head start, you can memorize them now. If you have trouble, remember that if you combine the first letter of each word, it will spell LDRSHIP.

Q: Since you mentioned these values, what else can I learn now to get ready for basic training?

A: In addition to reading this book and learning the Army Core Values there are some additional things you can do. Become familiar with the 24-hour clock, also known as military time. Memorize the enlisted and officer rank structure and be able to recognize the insignia. Look in Appendix B for some good websites for reference.

Q: So what are the graduation requirements?

A: Here they are in no certain order:

- Qualify with the M16A2 rifle
- Pass the Basic Physical Fitness Test
- Throw two live hand grenades and successfully complete the hand grenade qualification course
- Pass all performance oriented phase testing (such as the EOCT)
- Negotiate obstacles at the confidence and PECS courses
- Negotiate the bayonet assault course and participate in pugil-stick training
- Complete the gas chamber exercise to standard
- Complete 3,5,8,10 and 12k footmarches
- Participate in buddy team live-fire exercises
- Participate in hand-to-hand combat
- Participate in the final field training exercise
- Demonstrate understanding and a willingness to live the Army's seven core values
- Demonstrate the discipline, motivation and adherence to Army standards of conduct as a soldier

APPENDIX A—

BASIC TRAINING CURRICULUM

In order to better understand the different classes and periods of instruction (POIs) taught in basic training, the classes below are listed in alphabetical order. You will also find a general description of what the class or series of classes is about. All courses listed below are part of the Army Basic Training POI and must be taught according to regulation. Individual basic training posts may have some additional classes than those listed below. Basic training companies are also somewhat flexible in deciding how they put together their training schedules and what classes they will teach on what days of the cycle. Remember, that one company is competing for the same ranges and classrooms another company would like to have, as well as times in the dining facility and in other locations. This is why you will notice that training schedules are strictly adhered to. Drill sergeants only have nine weeks and limited resources to teach and run these classes, so keep this in mind when you feel overloaded with the information being taught!

Army Values: Basic Training revolves around the seven Army core values that include Loyalty, Duty, Respect, Selfless Service, Honor, Integrity and Personal Courage. Not only do soldiers have a class on the values, but they are constantly reminded of them throughout their training cycle.

Army Family Team Building (AFTB): This is an introduction to seeing the Army as a team. Family support groups, Army culture and rear detachments (parts of units left behind to take care of families' needs) are discussed.

Alcohol & Drug Prevention : The Army Alcohol and Drug Abuse Prevention and Control Program (ADAPCP) is introduced. Trainees learn the different choices of behavior and the consequences of abuse, as well as counseling and treatment resources available.

Basic Military Communications: Trainees learn the phonetic alphabet, use field telephones, send radio messages and use two types of radios: the VRC-12 series and the SINCGARS.

Basic Rifle Marksmanship: This program is divided into fourteen different periods of instruction. Students learn how the M16A2 functions, assemble/disassembly, zeroing the rifle, fundamentals of firing and cleaning, adjusting their sites, and have various opportunities to shoot at pop-up targets and to use the automated Weaponeer system. The Weaponeer is a computerized M16A2 with a screen, giving drill sergeants feedback on an individual trainee's shooting, potentially identifying any problems trainees may be having. Before soldiers shoot at the qualification range, they get a chance to practice the same sequence of pop-up targets. After qualification, soldiers fire with their protective masks on, fire the M16A2 in the burst mode (it does not fire on automatic, just three-round bursts) and at night with tracer bullets.

Bivouac: This is the trainees' first opportunity to set up their pup tents and spend one or two nights outside in the field. This is a non-tactical environment where soldiers learn basics of living outdoors and how to conduct personal hygiene in the field.

Code of Conduct: Students learn what is required of them in the event they are captured by the enemy. Not only is the Geneva Convention discussed, but also the aspects of captivity, survival, resistance and evasion techniques.

Conditioning Obstacle Course (PECS): An obstacle course soldiers negotiate individually, dressed in full combat gear. The course involves jumping, dodging, climbing and crawling. The course covers a few hundred yards and must be done quickly.

Conduct an Army Physical Fitness Session: Every Army unit conducts their physical fitness sessions in the same manner. Such things as setting up the formation to conduct exercises, the various exercises, games and fitness activites are taught. Soldiers throughout the Army use these stretching and muscle building exercises taught here, as well as the different exercises to build cardio-respiratory endurance.

Confidence Obstacle Course: A variety of difficult obstacles are negotiated; some are a group effort and others require an individual effort. Most obstacles are three to four stories high without safety nets. The course is designed to promote self-confidence, aggressiveness, daring and teamwork. Unlike the PECS, it is not a timed event. One favorite obstacle, seen in many movies, is the Inverted Rope Descent. Trainees climb up a high tower and crawl down a rope, feet first.

Daytime/Nighttime Defensive Firing: Trainees learn to fire from fighting positions (foxholes), during the day and at night. They learn how to support the foxhole position on their left and right with their own fire and how to adjust their aim using tracer bullets at night.

Diagnostic Basic Physical Fitness Test (BPFT): Within the first few days, a trainee's physical fitness level is tested. You must do push-ups, sit-ups and a two-mile run.

Drill & Ceremonies: This involves eight different periods of instruction. You learn the history of drill, stationary movements (such as standing at attention and parade rest), marching, drilling with your M16A2 Rifle, and drilling with a squad, platoon and company. The final event is the highly competitive platoon marching competition. In addition to the formal classes, trainees are frequently chosen to march company and platoon formations and learn some of their drill sergeants' favorite cadences in the process.

Environmental Awareness: Trainees are introduced to the Army's environmental program and how to be more sensitive to the environment, as well as learning hazardous waste disposal procedures.

Equal Opportunity: Trainees learn about discrimination, prejudice and harassment. Also discussed are the procedures used to report any problems of discrimination.

Field Training Exercise: A training exercise where you will spend three or four days outside in the field. You will sleep in your pup tent and conduct patrols and react to various threats. This is a tactical exercise where drill sergeants simulate a combat environment by using artillery, grenade, smoke and gas simulators.

Fire & Maneuver Course: A course where trainees move under simulated fire in buddy teams, shooting live rounds at pop-up targets while on the move. For safety reasons, you will wear a flak vest, as well as be accompanied by a drill sergeant down the firing lane.

First Aid: This includes eight different classes. Here, you learn the basics of first aid including: evaluating a casualty, restoring breathing, controlling bleeding, treating burns and fractures, learning preventive medicine, transporting a casualty and administering a nerve agent antidote.

Footmarches: You gradually increase the distance of the marches from 3 km to 20 km (This distance varies with the different training posts). Most marches are conducted to or from some of the ranges and trainees wear their rucksack, Kevlar helmet and carry their assigned rifle.

Guard Duty: This consists of two classes. The first class instructs a soldier on being a sentinel on guard and emphasizes the memorization of general and special orders (every soldier in the Army should be able to recite these). The second class involves dealing with an intruder or unknown person.

Healthy Lifestyles: Students learn the importance of good nutrition and diet, as well as the hazards of smoking and other unhealthy lifestyle choices.

Hand Grenades: Trainees identify the different types of grenades, learn different throwing techniques with practice grenades, negotiate a qualification course and throw two live hand grenades. This is potentially the most dangerous range trainees will encounter. The "boom" a live grenade makes is deafening and the shock wave has scared more than one private!

Hand-to-Hand Training: The aspects of hand to hand combat are taught. Soldiers are led through defensive and offensive moves, learn weak points of the attacker and how to fall properly.

Heritage & Traditions: The Army's rich heritage and traditions are introduced here. Most of the time, there is a sense of history in everything a soldier sees being done on a military post.

Identification and Wear of the Uniform: Trainees learn the different types of uniforms an Army soldier wears and how to properly wear them.

Individual Tactical Training: Soldiers move under fire, use teamwork in offensive and defensive situations and conceal themselves while on the move. Trainees also learn what objects provide adequate cover from the enemy's bullet. Most trainees enjoy putting on face camouflage in this class and there's typically one soldier who puts the leaves from what seems like an entire tree on his helmet.

Inspections: Throughout the cycle, Trainees must participate in a variety of inspections. A lot of time is spent cleaning one's personal equipment and assigned weapon. The trainee becomes very familiar with general knowledge questions related to the courses being taught, as well as basic military knowledge. During graduation week, the final and most important inspection is conducted by the company commander, first sergeant, battalion commander and the battalion command sergeant major.

Introduction to a Fitness Program: The components and principles of physical fitness and the proper method for calculation training heart rate are taught here.

Law of Land Warfare: Trainees become familiar with the principles of the Law of War and the Geneva-Hague Convention.

Map Reading: The world of military map reading and the use of a lensatic compass are taught in this series of classes. Trainees learn how to navigate with their compass and how to associate terrain with what they see on the map.

Military Customs & Courtesies: Many different individual tasks are taught here. Some are listed here. Soldiers are taught how to accompany a senior officer or enlisted soldier, report to an officer, react to an approaching officer or NCO and what to do when the national colors (American flag) are shown.

Military Justice: The laws and regulations of sexual conduct are taught, as well as an introduction to the Uniform Code of Military Justice (UCMJ). Additionally, the Army's policy on homosexual conduct is briefed.

Night Infiltration Course: Most trainees find this course the most exhilirating in basic training. They must crawl through an obstacle course with wire obstacles while simulated explosions are going off around them and live machinegun fire is being fired overhead.

Night Offensive Training: This is a course where trainees move as a part of a squad. They must react accordingly to machine gun fire and flares. This course is conducted in conjunction with the Night Infiltration Course.

Nuclear, Biological and Chemical Defense: Trainees learn how to care for and wear their protective mask, how to upgrade their protective level clothing, and how to use a decontamination kit. The use of chemical paper to detect liquid contaminants is also introduced. The most dreaded part of basic training is also included here, the gas chamber. Each trainee must enter the chamber and remove their mask. The purpose of this is to allow the soldier to gain confidence in their mask.

Personal Health & Hygiene: The Army health care system is introduced. Other topics include: hearing conservation, foot and body care, preventive medicine, self-examination for cancer (men and women), and the hazards of disease and infection in a field environment.

Phase Testing/End-of-Cycle Test (EOCT): At the end of Phase I and II, soldiers are tested, "hands-on", on a variety of tasks they learned in that phase. The EOCT is the culminating "hands-on" test taken towards the end of basic training. Trainees must pass this test, which usually has 20 tasks incorporating first aid, NBC defense, basic rifle marksmanship and a variety of other tasks. These are all covered in the IET Handbook.

Rifle Bayonet Training: Soldiers are taught offensive and defense movements with a bayoneted rifle. Trainees simulate bayonet fighting with each other, dressed in protective gear and using pugil sticks. An assault course is negotiated by the soldier and his assigned M16A2 rifle. This course consists of dummy targets that must be attacked and obstacles that must be negotiated as one moves along.

Safety: The basics on preventing cold and hot weather injuries are incorporated here.

Standards of Ethical Conduct: All government employees are held to certain standards of conduct, including those in the military. Here each soldier learns what is expected of him.

Sabotage & Espionage Directed Against the US Army (SAEDA): This is a briefing on recognizing and reporting subversion and espionage against the US Army.

Terrorism/Threat Orientation: Terrorism awareness is taught and soldiers learn to recognize enemy equipment, such as tanks and artillery pieces.

US Weapons: This is an introduction to other basic weapons the US Army uses. Included are the M249 Squad Automatic Weapon (the M60 Machine Gun is currently being phased-out in basic training), the AT4 Shoulder Fired Rocket, the M203 Grenade Launcher and the M18A1 Anti-personnel Mine. Every trainee is given the opportunity to fire all the weapons, except the anti-personnel mine. The mine's effectiveness is demonstrated by a trainee who is chosen from the company to accompany one of the instructors downrange to install and detonate it.

Unexploded Ordnance (UXO): This is a briefing on the hazards of unexploded bombs, explosives and other projectiles that one may find on the battlefield or training area. One is taught not to touch these items, as they might explode when handled.

Appendix B–

Useful
Basic Training Websites

Follow the links below to learn more about what you can do to prepare yourself. The website About.com has lots of extensive articles with great links, detailing what happens in all the Armed Forces basic training programs and how to prepare yourself. There is also a forum there to ask questions. The US Army Recruiting webpage also offers some assistance, as well as providing online chat schedules with recruiters. The Ft Leonard Wood, Ft Jackson, Ft Knox, Ft Sill and Ft Benning websites have links on how to prepare for basic training and what to bring. Just follow the "training" links on their homepages. While you are surfing these websites look for key words such as "POI" (Periods of Instruction) and "BCT" (Basic Combat Training). Ft Leonard Wood adds a nice touch, allowing you to look up training schedules of the individual companies and downloading photos of soldiers currently in training. You will also find a copy of the IET (Initial Entry Training) Handbook online. This book covers just about everything that you will encounter in basic training. It not only lists all the standards of the classes and descriptions of all the classes, but also details all the rules and regulations that govern basic training. If you want to know everything there is to know, then make sure to do a search for "Basic Training POI"! Lastly, if you still have questions and want even more information, you can come by my basic training website, join the discussion forum or send me an email!

•Army Basic Training (website by the author)
•http://www.armybasic.homestead.com

•About.com's US Military Forum
•http://forums.about.com/ab-usmilitary/messages

•US Army Recruiting Homepage
•http://www.goarmy.com

•Ft Leonard Wood Maneuver Support Center
•http://www.wood.army.mil

•US Army Training Center, Ft Jackson, SC
•http://jackson-www.army.mil/

•Ft Knox US Army Armor Center
•http://knox-www.army.mil/center/

•Ft Sill–Home of the Field Artillery
•http://sill-www.army.mil/

•Ft Benning Homepage–US Army Infantry School
•http://www.benning.army.mil/

- What's Hot at the US Army Physical Fitness School
- http://www-benning.army.mil/usapfs/WhatsHot/
  whatshotindex.htm

- Online Focus: Boot Camp Revisited–April 6, 1998
- http://www.pbs.org/newshour/bb/military/jan-june98/training_4-6.html

- Surviving Boot Camp
- http://www.usmilitary.about.com/careers/usmilitary/library/
  weekly/aa043000a.htm

- US Army Homepage
- http://www.army.mil/

- Army Rank Structure and Awards
- http://www-perscom.army.mil/tagd/tioh/rank/first.htm

- Military Basic Pay Charts
- http://www.dfas.mil/money/milpay/pay/bp-2.htm

- IET (Initial Entry Training) Handbook
- http://www.adtdl.army.mil/cgi-bin/atdl.dll/pam/600-4/tp600-4.htm

- Rite of Passage: Making Basic Training Tougher
- http://www.defenselink.mil/specials/basic/

- Boot Camp or Summer Camp?
- http://www.heritage.org/library/categories/natsec/bg1147.html

- Basic Training Tips
- http://www.thegillfam.com/basic.html

•Army Core Values at About.com
http://usmilitary.about.com/careers/usmilitary/library/milinfo/
blarvalues.htm

APPENDIX C–

TRAINING
SCHEDULE SNAPSHOT

The following section is intended to give you an idea of what is on the training schedule on nine separate days of the nine-week training cycle. I have randomly included a day from each week of training. These are actual training schedules that were used one Spring cycle while I was a basic training company commander. As you can see, every hour of your stay is filled with something to do! Not only are the classes and ranges listed on the schedules, but also meals, personal time and the times allowed for movement from one activity or class to another. Usually, if activities or classes are conducted in the company or battalion area, movement times are not annotated. "Movement" means that you march in formation from one activity to the next. "Movement by cattle truck" means that you are transported by these trucks to a range or other activity. Companies can also choose to march to and from some of the ranges, rather than using a "cattle truck". Sometimes you will notice that some time periods overlap, particularly during graduation week, where you may have half a company doing one activity while the other half does something else. To eliminate confusion, I have not included certain parts of the training schedules, as all the information can be pretty overwhelming. Other things typically listed on the training schedule are the individual sections doing the training (such as the entire company, platoon or selected individuals), the location, the instructor/trainer, references and the uniform. Each cadre member of a company carries a training schedule and current/upcoming schedules are also posted in the barracks for all to see. The word cadre is used to describe any member of a basic training unit or unit involved in the training of soldiers. Of course, your basic training cycle may vary somewhat, but all basic training companies are required to include all the courses and ranges in their schedule as listed in the Basic Combat Training Period of Instruction (POI). This POI is mandated by regulation and includes all the classes listed in the glossary.

Traditionally, before Week 1, every training company has what is called a "Fill Week". This "week", which can last as little as a day, is given the company to "fill" it with enough trainees to complete that cycle's group of trainees. For example, the basic training company due to start a cycle may not get enough trainees when it goes to "pick-up" soldiers at the reception station. Sometimes the reception station also gets behind in processing soldiers, so the basic training company has to have the flexibility to go back and get more trainees until they have their alloted number. The first official training day of the cycle then usually starts on a Friday.

Week 1 – Day 1

From	To	Subject
0001	0400	Lights Out
0400	0430	First Call

0430	0530	Class: Introduction to the Army Fitness Program
0530	0610	Personal Hygiene/Barracks Maintenance
0620	0720	Battalion In-processing
0720	0800	Breakfast
0800	0815	Movement
0815	0930	Class: Rights of the Accused/Court Martial
0930	1015	Battalion Commander Orientation
1015	1045	Chaplain Orientation
1045	1055	Break
1055	1125	Company Commander's Orientation
1125	1145	First Sergeant's Orientation
1145	1200	Battalion Sergeant Major's Orientation
1200	1220	Movement
1220	1300	Lunch
1300	1315	Movement
1315	1415	Class: Drill Orientation
1415	1645	Class: Individual Drill 1 – Stationary Movements
1645	1700	Movement
1700	1740	Dinner
1750	1850	Class: Healthy Lifestyles
1850	2000	Personal Time
1900	2000	Jewish Services (as applicable)
2000	2400	Lights Out

Week 2 – Day 13

0001	0400	Lights Out
0400	0430	First Call
0430	0530	Physical Fitness Training/Muscular Strength & Endurance
0530	0620	Personal Hygiene/Barracks Maintenance
0620	0640	Linen Turn-in

0640	0720	Breakfast
0720	0730	Movement
0730	1205	Class: First-Aid Day 2
1205	1220	Movement
1220	1300	Lunch
1300	1315	Movement
1315	1725	Class: First-Aid Day 2
1725	1740	Movement
1740	1820	Dinner
1820	1900	Drill Sergeant Time
1900	2000	Personal Time
2000	2400	Lights Out

Week 3 – Day 18

0001	0400	Lights Out
0400	0430	First Call
0430	0530	Physical Fitness Training/Cardio-Respiratory
0530	0610	Personal Hygiene/Barracks Maintenance
0620	0640	Weapons Issue
0640	0720	Breakfast
0720	0735	Movement
0735	0935	Class: Hand to Hand Combat – Stances and Strikes
0935	1145	Class: Hand to Hand Combat – Kicks, Falls and Throws
1145	1200	Movement
1200	1240	Lunch
1240	1300	Movement
1300	1500	Class: Platoon Drill
1500	1520	Movement
1520	1700	Class: Army Family Teambuilding
1700	1740	Dinner
1740	1830	Weapons Cleaning/Platoon Sergeant Time

1830	1900	Weapons Turn-in
1900	2000	Personal Time
2000	2400	Lights Out

Week 4 – Day 26

0001	0400	Lights Out
0400	0430	First Call
0430	0530	Physical Fitness Training/Cardio-Respiratory
0530	0610	Hygiene/Barracks Maintenance
0620	0640	Weapons Issue/Quartermaster Turn-in
0640	0720	Breakfast
0730	0800	Transportation by Cattle Truck
0800	1200	Range: Practice Record Fire I
1200	1300	Lunch (Field Chow)
1300	1630	Class: Establish a Bivouac Site
1630	1700	Transportation by Cattle Truck
1700	1740	Dinner
1750	1850	Weapons Cleaning
1900	1920	Weapons Turn-in
1920	2000	Personal Time
2000	2400	Lights Out

Week 5 – Day 32

0001	0400	Lights Out
0400	0430	First Call
0430	0530	Physical Fitness Training/Cardio-respiratory
0530	0610	Personal Hygiene/Barracks Maintenance
0610	0630	Weapons Issue/Linen Turn-in
0640	0720	Breakfast
0730	0800	Transportation by Cattle Truck
0800	1200	Range: US Weapons

HIE

1200	1300	Lunch (Field Chow)
1300	1700	Range: US Weapons
1700	1720	Transportation by Cattle Truck
1720	1800	Dinner
1810	1830	Weapons Turn-in
1830	1930	Drill Sergeant Time
1930	2000	Personal Time
2000	2400	Lights Out

Week 6 – Day 40

0001	0430	Lights Out
0430	0510	First Call/Personal Hygiene/Barracks Maintenance
0520	0600	Weapons Issue/Quartermaster Turn-in
0600	0640	Breakfast
0720	0750	Transportation by Cattle Truck
0750	1200	Individual Tactical Training
1200	1300	Lunch (Field Chow)
1300	1710	Individual Tactical Training
1710	1730	Transportation by Cattle Truck
1730	1830	Dinner (Field Chow)
1830	2130	Protective Mask Fire/Night Fire
2130	2200	Transportation by Cattle Truck
2200	2230	Weapons Cleaning/Turn-in
2230	2250	Personal Time
2250	2400	Lights Out

Week 7 – Day 46

0001	0430	Lights Out
0430	0500	First Call/Personal Hygiene
0500	0530	Barracks Maintenance
0540	0600	Weapons Issue/Quartermaster Turn-in
0600	0640	Breakfast

0640	0700	Movement
0700	1200	PECS Course
1200	1300	Lunch (Field Chow)
1300	1320	Movement
1320	1630	EOCT Reinforcement
1630	1700	Movement
1700	1750	Platoon Sergeant Time/Prep for Platoon Drill Competition
1800	1840	Dinner
1840	1900	Movement
1900	2000	Platoon Drill Competition
2000	2020	Movement
2020	2040	Weapons Turn-in
2040	2100	Personal Time
2100	2400	Lights Out

Week 8 – Day 50

0001	0500	Lights Out
0500	0550	First Call/Personal Hygiene/Barracks Maintenance
0600	0640	Breakfast
0640	0700	Weapons Issue
0700	0720	Transportation by Cattle Truck
0700	1200	End-of-Cycle Testing
1200	1300	Lunch (Field Chow)
1300	1700	End-of-Cycle Testing
1700	1720	Transportation by Cattle Truck
1720	1800	Weapons Turn-in
1850	2000	Personal Time
2000	2400	Lights Out

Week 9 – Day 61

0001	0430	Lights Out
0430	0500	First Call/Personal Hygiene/Barracks Maintenance
0500	0530	Preparation for Inspection 4 with the Battalion Commander
0540	0600	Weapons Issue
0600	0640	Breakfast
0650	1000	Preparation for Inspection 4 with the Battalion Commander
1000	1210	Battalion Commander Inspection (Inspection 4)
1220	1300	Lunch
1300	1320	Weapons Turn-in
1320	1350	Reverse pack TA-50
1340	1400	Movement for Key Personnel (as applicable)
1400	1500	Key Personnel Graduation Rehearsal
1400	1430	Transportation by Cattle Truck
1430	1630	Central Issue Facility (CIF) Turn-in
1630	1700	Transportation by Cattle Truck
1700	1900	Blood Drive (as applicable)
1700	1800	Battalion Commander Sensing Session
1700	1730	Platoon Sergeant Time
1740	1820	Dinner
1830	1900	Company Awards Ceremony Rehearsal
1900	2000	Personal Time
2000	2400	Lights Out

ABBREVIATIONS

AIT—Advanced Individual Training
AGR—Ability Group Run
APFT—Army Physical Fitness Test
BT—Basic Training
BCT—Basic Combat Training
BDU—Battle Dress Uniform
CIF–Central Issue Facility
CS Gas—Concentrated Smoke Gas
ELS—Entry Level Separation (Chapter 11)
EPTS—Existing Prior to Service (Chapter 5-11)
IET—Initial Entry Training
MRE—Meals Ready to Eat
NCO—Non-commissioned officer
PX—Post Exchange
RFT—Removed From Training

BIBLIOGRAPHY

TRADOC Regulation 350-6, *Initial Entry Training (IET) Policies and Administration*, Jan 21, 2000.

FLW Regulation 350-6, *Training Policies and Administration*, Dec 23, 1991.

RPI 925, *Guide for New Soldiers*, Sep 1993.

POI 21-114, *Army of Excellence Basic Combat Training Program of Instruction*, Oct 19, 1994.

FM 21-20, *Physical Fitness Training*, Sep 30, 1992.

Printed in the United States
2055